Meredith Levy

Interactive

Workbook 1 with Downloadable Audio

CAMBRIDGE
UNIVERSITY PRESS

CAMBRIDGE
UNIVERSITY PRESS

University Printing House, Cambridge CB2 8BS, United Kingdom

One Liberty Plaza, 20th Floor, New York, NY 10006, USA

477 Williamstown Road, Port Melbourne, VIC 3207, Australia

314–321, 3rd Floor, Plot 3, Splendor Forum, Jasola District Centre, New Delhi – 110025, India

103 Penang Road, #05-06/07, Visioncrest Commercial, Singapore 238467

Cambridge University Press is part of the University of Cambridge.

It furthers the University's mission by disseminating knowledge in the pursuit of
education, learning and research at the highest international levels of excellence.

www.cambridge.org
Information on this title: www.cambridge.org/9780521712095

First published 2011

20 19 18 17 16 15

Printed in Great Britain by CPI Group (UK) Ltd, Croydon CR0 4YY

A catalogue record for this publication is available from the British Library

ISBN 978-0-521-71209-5 Workbook with Downloadable Audio
ISBN 978-0-521-71208-8 Student's Book
ISBN 978-0-521-71210-1 Teacher's Book
ISBN 978-0-521-71211-8 Teacher's Resource Pack
ISBN 978-0-521-71214-9 Class Audio CDs
ISBN 978-0-521-14713-2 DVD (PAL)
ISBN 978-0-521-14720-0 DVD (NTSC)
ISBN 978-1-107-40213-3 Classware DVD-ROM
ISBN 978-1-107-40211-9 Testmaker CD-ROM and Audio CD

Contents

Quick Start

1

Write the plurals.

ruler	..rulers..............	family	....
rubber	....	phone	....
football	....	address	....
sandwich	....	dictionary	....

2

Follow the lines and make sentences.

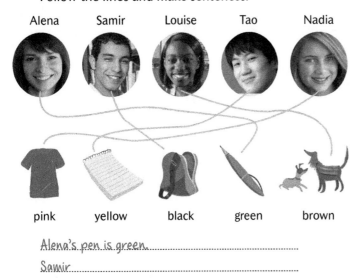

Alena   Samir   Louise   Tao   Nadia

pink   yellow   black   green   brown

Alena's pen is green......................................
Samir...
Louise...
Tao...
Nadia..

3

a **1** Listen and complete the information about two friends.

Name: Lena Petrova
Age: ¹........................... Class: 9C
Country: ²...........................
Mother's nationality: ³...........................
Father's nationality: ⁴...........................

Name: Ricardo Costa
Age: ⁵........................... Class: 9C
Country: ⁶...........................
Mother's nationality: ⁷...........................
Father's nationality: ⁸...........................

b Write the questions and answer them.

1 Lena / from Mexico?
   Is Lena from Mexico?......................
   No, she isn't. She's from Russia.........

2 her mother / Russian?
   ....
   ....
   ....

3 her friend's name / Roberto?
   ....
   ....
   ....

4 he / from Brazil?
   ....
   ....
   ....

5 Lena and Ricardo / 16?
   ....
   ....
   ....

6 they / in class 9C?
   ....
   ....
   ....

4

Complete the sentences. Use *There's* and *There are*.

1 There's a table... near the piano.
2 ....three ....on the table.
3 ....a .... under the table.
4 ....two .... on the floor.
5 ....a .... on the piano.

5

a Complete the table.

Subject pronouns	Object pronouns	Possessive adjectives
I	me	my
you	¹ *you*	7 ....
he	2	8 ....
she	3	9 ....
it	4	10 ....
we	5	11 ....
they	6	12 ....

b Read the sentences and complete the crossword.

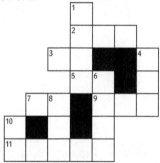

1 The children are in the garden. I can hear ....

2 That's Paul, near the door. Can you see .... ?

3 Hello, Mum. I'm at the park and Josh is with ....

4 Rosa's brother is eight and .... sister is twelve.

5 Hi! .... name's Leah. Nice to meet you.

6 I'd like to write to you. What's .... email address?

7 Those are our books. Give them to .... , please.

8 Anna is my friend. .... 's in my class at school.

9 Dad and I have got blonde hair and .... eyes are blue.

10 I can see your phone. .... 's on the floor.

11 He's got two sisters. .... names are Amira and Laila.

6

Make sentences with *has got* and *have got*.

Our cat	~~These girls~~	Those men
That house	My father	

a new computer	big eyes	~~long hair~~
very good bikes	a swimming pool	

1 *These girls have got long hair.*

2 ....
....
....

3 ....
....
....

4 ....
....
....

5 ....
....
....

7

Answer these questions.

1 Can you play the piano?

   Yes, I can. / No, I can't.

2 Can a fish walk?

   ....

3 Can you write in Chinese?

   ....

4 Can you ride a bike?

   ....

5 Can your friend speak Turkish?

   ....

6 Can dogs swim?

   ....

Grammar reference: pages 78, 80, 82, 96

1 Vocabulary

Family

a Write the names on Matt's family tree.

```
1 ................... = Charles

2 ................... = Joanna          3 ................... = 4 ...................

5 ...................        Matt        6 ...................
```

My name's Matt. My parents are Joanna and Evan, and I've got a sister called Ellie. My grandfather's name is Charles and my grandmother is Lucy. My uncle Tom is my mother's brother and his wife is called Sophie. Ben is their son – he's my cousin.

b Complete the sentences with words for members of the family.

1 Matt is Ellie's _brother_ .
2 Ellie is Evan's ....
3 Charles is Ben's ....
4 Sophie is Matt's ....
5 Joanna is Tom's ....
6 Evan is Joanna's ....
7 Tom is Lucy's ....
8 Matt and Ellie are Ben's ....

c Complete the sentences. Use the word in the box.

1 Kate is Adam's sister.

   | brother |

   Adam _is Kate's brother._

2 Helen is Sara's mother.

   | daughter |

   Sara ....

3 Jack is Paula's husband.

   | wife |

   Paula ....

4 Tomas and Maria are my parents.

   | husband |

   Tomas ....

5 Karen's parents are my aunt and uncle.

   | cousin |

   Karen .... my ....

6 My mother is Ann and her father's name is Max.

   | grandfather |

   Max ....

7 Yusuf is my uncle and Fatima is his wife.

   | aunt |

   Fatima ....

2 Grammar Grammar reference: page 84

Present simple: *I/you/we/they*

a Put the words in the correct order.

1 like / friends / I / Robert's / really
   I really like Robert's friends.

2 school / don't / to / We / walk
   ....
   ....

3 in / Irena's / live / a / brothers / flat
   ....
   ....

4 Julie / got / little / called / a / I've / sister
   ....
   ....

5 with / every / have dinner / We / Sunday / our grandmother
   ....
   ....

6 got / friends / My / any pets / haven't
   ....
   ....

7 to / They / us / don't / with / go out / want
   ....
   ....

b Complete the sentences. Use the positive or negative form of the verbs in the box.

| want | ~~drive~~ | live | speak | work | write |

1 People ..drive.. on the left in the UK.
2 I .... to buy this CD. It's great!
3 My parents work from Monday to Friday. They
   .... at the weekend.

4 I .... emails because I haven't got
   a computer.
5 Sam's cousins live in Switzerland. They
   .... French and German.
6 Lydia and her family .... in Italy.
   Their house is in Athens.

c Look at the pictures and complete the sentences.

1 I .live.in.a.flat.. in Madrid.
2 You ....
3 We ....

4 They .... on Sundays.
5 I .... every evening.
6 They .... by bus.

③ Vocabulary

Everyday things

a Put the boxes in order and make ten words.

icyc	V mob	~~aper k~~	le ph
~~newsp~~	rella	ock b	mera T
mp umb	oto la	ile cl	eys ca

1 .newspaper.... 5 .... 8 ....
2 .k.................. 6 .... 9 ....
3 .... 7 .... 10 ....
4 ....

b Complete the sentences. Use the singular or plural form of the words in Exercise 3a.

In this room there's a small ¹.TV..., a ²........................ ,
a big ³........................ and an ⁴........................ . There
are two ⁵........................ and three ⁶........................ .
There are also some old ⁷........................ on the table
and some ⁸........................ on the floor. There isn't a
⁹........................ and there aren't any ¹⁰........................ .

④ Pronunciation

The schwa /ə/ at the end of words

a 🔊 2 Listen to the /ə/ sound at the end
of the words.

father   dollar   cinema

b 🔊 3 Listen and (circle) the words with
/ə/ and a consonant at the end. Listen again
and repeat.

parent   husband   cousin   Japan
computer   children   Poland   weekend
open   email   pilot

c 🔊 4 Listen and practise saying these
sentences.

I've got a sister and a brother.
Her mother and father are German.
Anna's cousins are from England.

> **Practise saying these words**
>
> 🔊 5 aunt   because   bicycle
> country   daughter   email   evening
> favourite   language   listen   watch
> work

(5) Grammar Grammar reference: page 84

Present simple: questions

a Match the two parts of the questions.

1	D	Do your	A	your cousins live?
2		Do	B	your favourite singer?
3		Do your friends play	C	have for breakfast?
4		When do you	D	grandparents work?
5		Where do	E	your brother's name?
6		What do you	F	computer games?
7		What is	G	you like dogs?
8		Who is	H	watch TV?

b 🔊 6 Write two words to complete each question. Then listen and check.

A: ¹ <u>Where do</u> you live?

B: In Liverpool.

A: ² _____ _____ English?

B: No, I'm not. I'm from Poland.

A: ³ _____ _____ study English at school?

B: Yes, I do.

A: ⁴ _____ you _____ in a house or a flat?

B: In a flat.

A: ⁵ _____ _____ you do after school?

B: I go to my friend's house and we listen to music.

A: ⁶ _____ _____ your favourite sports?

B: Football and tennis.

c Write questions about Maria using the verbs. Then write her answers.

1 you / music on the radio? (listen)

<u>Do you listen to music on the radio?</u>

<u>Yes, I do.</u>

2 you / the newspaper in the morning? (read)

....

....

3 your friends / to school? (walk)

....

....

4 When / your lessons? (start)

....

....

5 Where / your grandparents? (live)

....

....

6 Read

Read Oliver's profile and answer the questions.

File   Edit   View   History   Bookmarks   Window   Help

About me

My name's Oliver. I'm 14 years old and I'm British. I live in a small house in London with my parents and my brothers, Harry and Tim. Our dog is called Jessie and we've got a cat and two rabbits. It's always noisy in our house because people from our family come to visit all the time. My grandparents' house is next to ours so we see them every day, and my uncle and aunt often come for dinner with my three cousins.

My friends are Karl and Amir and we love computers. We've got our own website with lots of photos and videos on it. We also read computer magazines, and after school we play computer games. My school is called Melrose College, but Karl and Amir go to Forest Vale School.

1 What country does Oliver come from?

The UK.

2 Where is his house?

3 How many boys are there in the family?

4 How many pets have they got?

5 Do Oliver's grandparents live in a flat or a house?

6 Who are Karl and Amir?

7 What do Oliver and his friends do in the afternoon on school days?

8 Do the three boys all go to different schools?

(7) Listen

7 A girl wants to join a club. Listen and complete the information.

First name:	1
Surname:	2
Age:	3
Nationality:	4
Languages:	5
	6
Favourite activities:	films
	7
	8

Portfolio 1

Complete the form with your information.

File　　Edit　　View　　History　　Bookmarks　　Window　　Help

EMAIL ADDRESS:

FIRST NAME:

SURNAME:

COUNTRY:

PERSONAL PROFILE

FAVOURITE MUSIC:

FAVOURITE TV PROGRAMMES:

FAVOURITE FILMS:

FAVOURITE BOOKS:

ABOUT ME:

Quiz ①

a What do you remember about Unit 1? Answer all the questions you can and then check in the Student's Book.

1 Where is Nairobi?

....

2 Look at picture A. Which sentence is not true?

A They live in a house. ☐

B They haven't got a pet. ☐

C They live in Beijing. ☐

3 Why are Japanese names unusual?

....

4 Complete the word pairs.

wife .... son ....

uncle ....

5 Who is your mother's sister's son?

....

6 There are two mistakes in these sentences. Write the correct sentences.

Speak you English?

Yes, I speak.

....

....

7 What are the three things in picture B?

....

....

8 Name two things you can use to take photos.

....

9 Name three types of pet in Unit 1.

....

....

10 Which four words end with the /ə/ sound?

newspaper magazine Kenya dinner family grandmother

....

....

b 🔊 8 Listen and check.

c Now look at your Student's Book and write two more quiz questions for Unit 1.

Question: ....
....
Answer: ....

Question: ....
....
Answer: ....

2 A day in my life

① Vocabulary

Daily activities

a Match the words (1–10) and the activities (A–J).

1	[B] get	**A**	school
2	[ ] have	**B**	up
3	[ ] go out with	**C**	online
4	[ ] go to	**D**	music
5	[ ] do	**E**	dressed
6	[ ] go	**F**	my homework
7	[ ] go	**G**	breakfast
8	[ ] get	**H**	to bed
9	[ ] have a	**I**	my friends
10	[ ] listen to	**J**	shower

b

Write the activities.

1 _get up_

2 ....
....

3 ....
....

4 ....
....

5 ....
....

6 ....
....

② Grammar Grammar reference: page 84

Present simple: *he/she/it*

> **Check it out!**
>
> **Spelling of -s endings**
>
> Verbs ending in *-s*, *-sh*, *-ch* or *-o*: add *-es*.
> miss**es**   finish**es**   watch**es**   do**es**
>
> Verbs ending in a consonant + *-y*: change to *-ies*.
> stud**y** → stud**ies**

a Complete the sentences with the verbs in the present simple.

1 Natalie _writes_ (write) lots of emails.
2 Dad .... (buy) a newspaper every morning.
3 Jane often .... (go) to the cinema at the weekend.
4 My brother .... (finish) work at 5:00.
5 Mrs Lawson .... (teach) French and German at our school.
6 Omar .... (have) lunch with his friends at 12:30.
7 Kate's mother .... (study) Spanish in evening classes.

b Complete the text with these verbs in the present simple.

have	go	play	~~get up~~	not be	not start	not like

Francesca ¹ _gets up_ early every morning and she
² .... to the swimming pool for an hour.
After her swim, she ³ .... a shower and
gets dressed for school. She ⁴ .... Maths
or Science and she ⁵ .... very good at
languages, but she loves PE. She ⁶ ....
her homework until eight o'clock in the evening because
she ⁷ .... basketball after school.

c Look at the picture of Jason. Write questions and answers about him.

1 live / in Rome?

Does he live in Rome?

No, he doesn't.

2 Where / live?

....

....

3 play / football?

....

....

4 walk / to school?

....

....

5 How / go / to school?

....

....

6 What / do / on the bus?

....

....

③ Vocabulary

School subjects

a Find nine more school subjects in the puzzle. Match them with the pictures.

G	N	L	P	M	U	S	I	C
O	E	T	E	R	A	K	W	U
S	F	O	Z	E	R	T	O	H
C	E	N	G	L	I	S	H	I
I	L	U	A	R	Y	E	B	S
E	M	I	R	D	A	I	R	T
N	A	X	T	L	V	P	U	O
C	H	F	R	E	N	C	H	R
E	L	O	S	I	C	T	D	Y

$x^2 + y^2 = z$

1 PE............ **2** .... **3** .... **4** .... **5** ....

6 .... **7** .... **8** .... **9** .... **10** ....

b Write true answers to these questions.

1 How many Science lessons do you have every week?

....

2 Do you think Maths is difficult?

....

3 Do you study History and Geography at school?

....

4 When is your next English lesson?

....

5 What other languages can you study at your school?

....

6 What is your first lesson on Monday morning?

....

7 What is your last lesson of the week?

....

④ Listen

a 🔊 9 Listen to the conversation from a radio programme. Write the two missing times in the school timetable.

b 🔊 9 Listen again and complete the timetable (1–5).

MONDAY	
.............–9:40	1 ....
9:40–10:20	Maths
10:20–10:40	break
10:40–11:20	Art
11:20–12:00	2 ....
12:00–1:00	3 ....
1:00–1:40	4 ....
1:40–2:15	History
2:15–2:35	break
2:35–3:10	5 ....
3:10–.............	Science

⑤ Grammar Grammar reference: page 84

Adverbs of frequency

a Rewrite the sentences with the adverbs.

1 We go shopping on Saturday morning. (often)
   ..We often go shopping on Saturday morning...

2 I have a shower after school. (sometimes)
   ....

3 Dogs are friendly. (usually)
   ....

4 Chris watches TV in the morning. (never)
   ....

5 Martin finishes his homework. (hardly ever)
   ....

6 Nicole is on the phone. (always)
   ....

b There are mistakes in each sentence. ~~Cross out~~ the wrong word(s) and write the correct word(s).

1 My friend Daniela ~~walks usually~~ home with me.
   ..usually walks..............

2 I see often Tarek because he goes to my school.
   ....

3 My aunt sometime has lunch with us on Sunday.
   ....

4 Suzie always is in bed before midnight.
   ....

5 My brothers aren't hardly ever at home.
   ....

6 David never doesn't go to the cinema.
   ....

c Look at the information about Lisa's typical week. Write sentences with adverbs of frequency.

	Mon	Tue	Wed	Thu	Fri	Sat	Sun
1 get up / early	✓		✓		✓		
2 do / homework	✓	✓	✓	✓	✓	.	✓
3 have / shower	✓	✓	✓	✓	✓	✓	✓
4 be / late for school							
5 go / online	✓	✓		✓	✓		✓
6 go / bed early	✓						

1 *She sometimes gets up early.*

2 ....

3 ....

4 ....

5 ....

6 ....

Present simple: all forms

d 🔊 **10** Choose the correct answer: A, B or C. Then listen and check.

Joe: So here we are – waiting for Laura again. Where is she?

Eleni: I [1]....... know.

Joe: Why [2]....... late?

Eleni: Joe, you know she [3]....... a music lesson after school on Fridays.

Joe: But her class [4]....... at six. It's five to eight now.

Eleni: Well, she goes home and has a shower – you know. Anyway, here she is now.

Laura: Hi, [5]....... late? When [6]....... ?

Eleni: It's OK. It [7]....... start until 8 o'clock.

Laura: Oh, good. I want to get something to eat.

Joe: No! We [8]....... got time. Come on, let's go!

1 **A** can't   **(B)** don't   **C** doesn't

2 **A** she's always   **B** always is she   **C** is she always

3 **A** have   **B** does have   **C** has

4 **A** usually finish   **B** usually finishes   **C** finishes usually

5 **A** am I   **B** I'm   **C** do I

6 **A** the film starts   **B** is the film start   **C** does the film start

7 **A** doesn't   **B** never   **C** always

8 **A** doesn't   **B** haven't   **C** don't

(6) Pronunciation

Words with /z/

a 🔊 **11** Listen and (circle) the /z/ sounds in the words. Then listen again and repeat.

1 She goes out.

2 He stays at home.

3 She has a shower.

4 He travels in Spain.

5 Susan is a student.

b 🔊 **12** Listen and (circle) the /z/ sounds in the sentences.

1 My cousin plays and sings in a band.

2 Zoë always has History on Tuesdays.

3 Sam doesn't like his music lessons.

4 Does your sister send emails to her friends?

Practise saying these words

🔊 **13** breakfast   foreign   Geography   half   never   quarter   Science   shower   sometimes   special   subject   usually

(7) Read

a Read the article. Are sentences 1–6 right (✓) or wrong (✗)?

Home schooling

In the UK and other countries some students never go to school. Instead, they learn at home with their parents. This is called home schooling.

In the Davis family, Emily Davis stays at home and teaches her daughter Nadia (14) and her son Robbie (12). They don't have a timetable, but in a typical week they start at about 9:00 and work for three or four hours before lunch.

In the afternoon they do lots of different things. Nadia says: 'I sometimes go online or I write music, or maybe I cook something with Mum. But we often go out too. We visit lots of different places. Sometimes we meet up with other home-schoolers. Sometimes we just go shopping or to the swimming pool.'

'All children want to learn,' Emily says. 'But in a school teachers can't give time to every student. I can give lessons that are interesting for my children. I can't answer all their questions on every subject, but it's easy to find the information they want. We often learn together – that's good for me too!'

1 The UK is the only place that has home schooling. ☐

2 Emily Davis is a schoolteacher. ☐

3 Nadia and Robbie usually have lessons at home in the morning. ☐

4 They don't always stay at home in the afternoon. ☐

5 They hardly ever see other teenagers during the day. ☐

6 Home schooling is boring for Emily. ☐

b Do you like the idea of home schooling? Prepare to talk about this in your next class. Make notes to help you.

....

....

....

Help yourself!

and, but and because

Remember to use link words to join your ideas.

Complete these sentences with *and*, *but* and *because*.

1 I love pasta, ... I don't like rice.

2 We haven't got any pets .... we live in a small flat.

3 Manuel's a good singer .... he also plays the guitar.

Portfolio 2

Describe your school for an internet web page. Write two paragraphs.

1 **General information**
- Where is the school?
- How many students are there?
- How old are the students?

2 **Lessons**
- When does the school day start and finish?
- What subjects do all students study?
- What other subjects can students study?

Quiz 2

a What do you remember about Unit 2? Answer all the questions you can and then check in the Student's Book.

B

C

1 Look at picture A. Where does the girl come from?

....

2 Why doesn't the girl in picture A go to school?

....

3 Make three activities. Use a word from each box.

| get | go to | go | online | dressed | bed |

....

....

7 This school subject teaches you to draw and paint. What is it?

....

4 What is the first meal of the day?

....

8 What is the school subject in picture C?

....

5 Look at picture B. What does the boy do at 7.30?

He ....

and he ....

9 Put the words in the correct order.

games / ever / Adam / plays / hardly / computer

....

....

6 There are two mistakes in these sentences. Write the correct sentences.

A: Is Sara live in Poland?

B: No, she isn't.

....

....

10 Put these words in the correct place: *usually, often, sometimes.*

A   B   C   D   E   F

A never   D ....

B hardly ever   E ....

C ....   F always

b 🔊 **14** Listen and check.

c Now look at your Student's Book and write two more quiz questions for Unit 2.

Question: ....
....

Answer: ....

Question: ....
....

Answer: ....

① Grammar Grammar reference: page 86

Present continuous

> **Check it out!**
>
> **Spelling of -ing words**
>
> Don't forget the spelling rules.
>
> Verbs ending in -e:
> ride → riding   have → having
>
> Verbs ending in -ie:
> lie → lying
>
> Verbs ending in one vowel + a consonant: double the consonant.
> swim → swimming   get → getting

a Write the -ing form of the verbs.

1 write

...writing............................

2 drink

....

3 go

....

4 shop

....

5 read

....

6 run

....

7 make

....

8 sit

....

b Complete the sentences with the verb *be*.

1 My friends ..are.. having lunch at the beach.

2 Kate .... visiting her aunt in Scotland.

3 My parents are cooking. They .... sunbathing.

4 I .... really enjoying this book. It isn't very interesting.

5 Where .... your friend staying at the moment?

6 .... you learning German this year?

c 🔊 15 Look at the pictures and correct the sentences. Then listen and check.

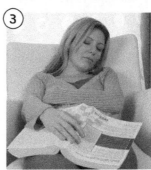

1 Is Jamie taking a photo on his phone?

.No, he isn't. He's talking.......................

2 Are Joe and Ali swimming?

....

3 Is Mum reading her book?

....

....

4 Are you playing a computer game?

....

....

5 Are the girls walking on the beach?

....

....

6 Is he sitting in the café?

....

....

....

2 Vocabulary

Holiday activities

… an ice cream

… souvenirs

a Write words 1–9 in the puzzle. Then use the eight ◯ letters to make one more holiday activity.

1 ⓈU R F
2
3
4
5
6
7
8
9

☐ L ☐ ☐ ☐ ☐ ☐ ☐ ☐

… to a disco

… a horse

CLICK!
… photos

b Complete the sentences with the words/phrases in Exercise 2a.

1 You ride a board on the water when you ..surf.. .

2 If you want to dance, you can ....

3 If you want something to eat at the cinema, you can ....

4 When people .... , they sleep in a tent.

5 You need a camera to ....

6 When people are on holiday, they often .... for their friends.

7 You can .... in a pool or in the sea.

8 People don't .... in the winter.

9 When you .... , you sit on its back.

3 Grammar

Grammar reference: page 84 and page 86

Present simple and present continuous

Circle the correct words.

1 *I never go* / *I'm never going* to bed before 10 o'clock.

2 How *do you spell* / *are you spelling* your name?

3 Tim isn't here right now. *He stays* / *He's staying* with some friends in London.

4 Jess is at a sports camp this week. *She has* / *She's having* a good time and *she learns* / *she's learning* to ride a horse.

5 What *do they say* / *are they saying*? *I don't speak* / *I'm not speaking* Russian.

6 I don't think Patrick *works* / *is working* at the moment. *I don't know* / *I'm not knowing* where he is.

7 A: Hi, Jackie. What *do you do* / *are you doing*?

B: *I write* / *I'm writing* an article for the school newspaper, but *I don't think* / *I'm not thinking* it's very good. *Do you want* / *Are you wanting* to read it?

4 Read

Read the information and complete the table with a tick (✓) or a cross (✗).
Find the name of the girl in the photo.

I'm on a camping holiday with a group of friends and I'm having a great time. We go to the beach every day and I'm learning to water-ski. My favourite place to eat is the café at the Plaza Hotel – the food there is lovely!

	🏕	🏖	🏄	🪑
Helen		✓		
Julia				
Sara				

The girl's name is ....

- Helen is having a holiday with some friends at the beach.
- Julia usually stays with her aunt, but this year she's camping with some friends.
- Swimming is Sara's favourite activity, and she always goes to the beach during the holidays.
- Helen's holiday flat is near the Plaza Hotel.
- There's a nice café in the hotel and Helen often has lunch there.
- Julia goes swimming in the sea every day.
- Sara is sharing a tent with two other girls.
- Someone is teaching Julia how to water-ski while she's on holiday.
- Helen doesn't go in the water because she can't swim.
- Sara is learning a new sport – she's having lessons with Julia.
- Julia loves the Plaza Café, but she doesn't eat there every day.
- Sara never goes out for lunch or dinner because she hasn't got much money.

5 Vocabulary

Weather and temperature

> **Check it out!**
>
> **Spelling of -y adjectives**
>
> Nouns that end with one vowel + a consonant: double the consonant + -y.
>
> *sun → sunny*

a Put the letters in the correct order to make weather words. Then write the adjectives.

1 nus

...sun............... ....sunny............

2 dniw

....

3 nira

....

4 ogf

....

5 swon

....

6 ludoc

....

b Match these words/phrases with the pictures.

cool   hot   really hot   cold   warm   freezing

1 ....   2 ....

3 ....   4 ....

5 ....   6 ....

c What is the weather like in these cities?

Rio de Janeiro: _In Rio de Janeiro it's hot_

and sunny.

New York: _____

_____

Istanbul: _____

_____

Moscow: _____

_____

Nairobi: _____

_____

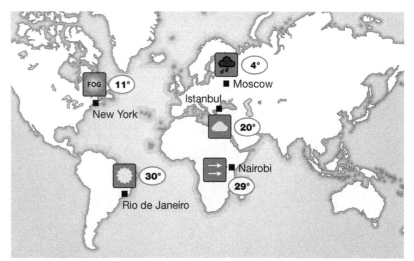

FOG 11° New York

Moscow 4°

Istanbul 20°

Nairobi 29°

Rio de Janeiro 30°

Help yourself!

Compound nouns (1)

In English, two words often join together to make a new compound word.

week|end   foot|ball   pen|friend   lunch|time

Can you join these words to make six compound nouns? Write them under the pictures.

sun...	man	glasses	coat	cream
rain...	forest	~~ball~~		
snow...				

1 _snowball_   2 _____

3 _____   4 _____

5 _____   6 _____

Write these words in your notebook.
Look in your English dictionary and find some other weather compounds you can add.

6 Pronunciation

Two-syllable words ending in /ə/

a Remember, lots of words have the sound /ə/ in English:

Chin**a**   moth**er**   par**e**nt   Lond**o**n

Follow the words ending in a syllable with /ə/ to find a way through the puzzle.

→ summer	disco	city	fifteen	football
weather	subject	winter	breakfast	England
autumn	picture	German	English	centre
email	swimming	sunbathe	million	teacher
cloudy	music	weekend	Poland	surname
finish	sometimes	early	famous	never →

b 🔊 16 Listen and check.

c 🔊 17 Listen and practise saying these sentences.

Robert often doesn't listen to the teacher.

The weather in Russia is warm at the moment.

Practise saying these words

🔊 18 afternoon   design   different
enjoy   learn   mountain   phone
right   sunbathe   warm   weather
world

(7) Listen

🔊 **19** Listen to Sam talking about his holiday. Tick (✓) the correct answer: A, B or C.

1 Where is Sam staying?

A ☐   B ✓   C ☐

4 Who is having something to eat?

father   mother   sister

A ☐   B ☐   C ☐

2 What's the weather like?

A ☐   B ☐   C ☐

5 How is Sam feeling?

A ☐   B ☐   C ☐

3 What is Sam doing now?

A ☐   B ☐   C ☐

Portfolio 3

Look at the advert. Imagine you are on holiday at the Paradise Beach Hotel. Write a short letter to a friend. Tell him/her what you do there and what you are doing now. Here are some expressions you can use:

I'm/We're staying …
At the moment I'm …
Every day/morning I/we …
We often/usually …
It's nice/beautiful/fun/boring.

Paradise Beach Hotel
★ ★ ★

24 rooms
Swimming pool
Restaurant and café
Internet facilities

Activities
• swimming • surfing • windsurfing • walking • tennis • dancing
And lots more!

Quiz 3

a What do you remember about Unit 3? Answer all the questions you can and then check in the Student's Book.

A

1 What type of camp are Luke and Molly staying in?
....

2 Which country are Luke and Molly in?
....

B

3 In Britain the word is *football*. What is the American word?
....

7 Where can people go to swim, surf and sunbathe?
....

4 There are two mistakes in this sentence. Write the correct sentence.
I having a good time at the camp, but Nick doesn't enjoying it.
....
....
....

8 What is the weather like in picture B?
....

9 Circle the adjective that is different.
cool   warm   freezing   cold

5 Which of these words has the wrong spelling? Write the correct spelling.
drinking   shareing   shopping   going
....

10 Underline two verbs that are not correct in this sentence.

I'm not	reading	this book.
	wanting	
	buying	
	understanding	
	enjoying	

6 What is the girl doing in picture A?
....

b 🔊 20 Listen and check.

c Now look at your Student's Book and write two more quiz questions for Unit 3.

Question: ....
....
Answer: ....

Question: ....
....
Answer: ....

4 Sport crazy

1 Vocabulary

Sports

a Complete the crossword. Use the clues to help you.

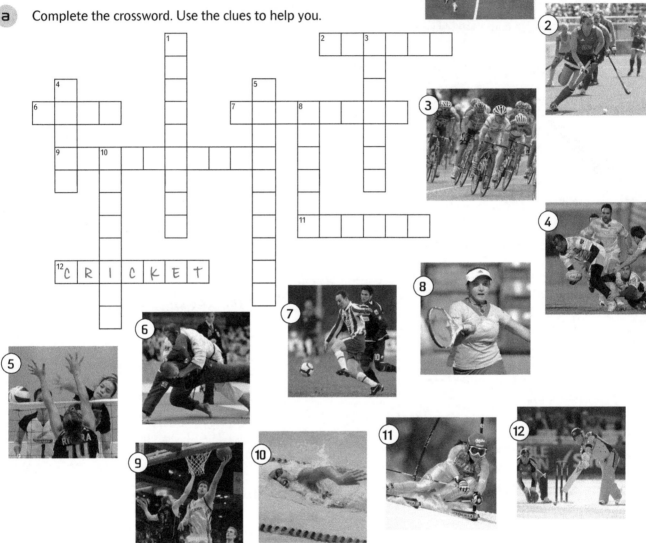

b Write the sports from the crossword in the correct list.

play: cricket ....

....

go: ....

do: ....

c 🔊 21 Complete the sentences with phrases in Exercise 1b. Then listen and check.

1 You need two teams of 11 players to ..play cricket.. .

2 People .... in the mountains in the winter.

3 You can .... with two or four players.

4 When you ...., you try to throw the other person on the floor.

5 People ride bikes when they ....

6 Players in each team jump up and hit the ball with their hands when they ....

(2) Grammar Grammar reference: page 88

Verb + -ing

a Rewrite the sentences using the -ing form of the verbs in the box.

> listen to   play   ~~study~~   do   drink   watch

1 I don't like French.

.....I don't like studying French.....

2 We like films.

....

3 I love hot chocolate.

....

4 Kate really enjoys athletics.

....

5 Daniel hates basketball.

....

6 My parents don't like pop music.

....

....

b Write sentences with *enjoy, like, not like, love* and *hate*.

1 Ian ...loves singing................................... .

2 Janek ....

3 Adam ....

4 Ayesha ....

5 Jill ....

c Use the table to write five true sentences.

I	like not like love hate	get up play do take talk watch go	photos to school tennis sport on TV to my friends on the phone homework at the weekend computer games early in the morning athletics

.....I don't like playing tennis.....

1 ....

2 ....

3 ....

4 ....

5 ....

(3) Pronunciation

/ŋ/

a 🔊 22 (Circle) the three words that do not have the /ŋ/ sound. Then listen, check and repeat.

thing   thin   sing   singer   cinema   drink
drinking   think   thinking   begin   England   English

b 🔊 23 Listen and tick (✓) the phrase you hear. Then listen again and repeat.

1 [✓] come in   [ ] coming
2 [ ] go into the house [ ] going to the house
3 [ ] swim in a pool   [ ] swimming pool
4 [ ] write in a book   [ ] writing a book
5 [ ] an interest in sport [ ] an interesting sport

c 🔊 24 Listen and practise saying these sentences.

He's coming.
It's raining.
She's studying this evening.
I'm going to the swimming pool.
I think they're speaking English.

Practise saying these words

🔊 25 airport   athletics   basketball
college   cycling   famous   football   organise
skiing   stadium   travel   women

---

4 Vocabulary

Sports words

a Find five more words for actions you can do with a ball in the word snake.

FATHROWERHITARKICKYGABOUNCENRPICKUPANCATCHEL

1 throw_____
2 _____
3 _____
4 _____
5 _____
6 _____

b Are these sentences right (✓) or wrong (✗)?

1 Footballers kick the ball. ☐
2 Basketball players don't throw the ball. ☐
3 In a rugby game, players can't pick up the ball. ☐
4 Players don't hit the ball when they play tennis. ☐
5 You can bounce the ball in a basketball game. ☐
6 In hockey, only one player in the team can catch the ball. ☐

5 Grammar   Grammar reference: page 88

Adverbs of manner

a <u>Underline</u> the verbs in these sentences. Then complete the sentences with adverbs.

1 The class <u>is reading</u> ..quietly.. (quiet) in the library.
2 Listen _____ (careful) to this message!
3 My brother is working _____ (hard) in his new job.
4 Trains travel very _____ (quick) from Paris to London.
5 Suzie plays tennis really _____ (good).
6 Manchester United are winning _____ (easy).

b Write sentences about the people in pictures 1–5. Use adverbs for the adjectives in the box.

noisy   good   ~~careful~~   fast   slow

1 He's writing carefully._____

2 It_____

3 They_____

4 He_____

5 _____

6 Listen

a 🔊 26 Listen to three people talking about sports. Tick (✓) the sports you hear.

basketball ☐	golf ☐	swimming ☐	football ☐
cricket ☐	hockey ☐	tennis ☐	skiing ☐
cycling ☐	judo ☐	volleyball ☐	

b 🔊 26 Listen again. Write the two sports that each person likes playing.

1 Isabel likes:

....

....

2 Andrew likes:

....

....

3 Silvia likes:

....

....

(7) Read

Read Leo's report about his favourite sport. Choose the correct answer: A, B or C.

school sports club news

Water polo is a new sport at our school, but we've got a good team now. We practise after school on Thursdays at the Northside Pool and we're doing well in the National Schools Competition.

There are seven players in a water polo team. The game is a bit like football because each team tries to score goals with a ball. But in water polo you don't use your feet – you catch and throw the ball with one hand. And you never stop swimming. A game lasts 32 minutes, and in that time you swim up and down a 30-metre pool lots of times. If you aren't fit, water polo isn't the sport for you!

For me it's great, because I love being in the water and I can swim fast. I also really enjoy being part of a team. We've got some excellent players and we're all good friends. So it's fun, and it's also a fantastic way to get fit.

Leo Johnson

File   Edit   View   History   Bookmarks   Window   Help

1 People play water polo
  A in a stadium.
  B in a swimming pool.
  C at the beach.

2 Leo plays this sport
  A every week.
  B in the morning.
  C with seven other players.

3 His team plays
  A well.
  B badly.
  C in a new competition.

4 Water polo players
  A often play football.
  B bounce the ball.
  C don't kick the ball.

5 In a water polo game, players
  A can't use their hands.
  B sometimes swim 30 metres.
  C swim all the time.

6 Leo
  A isn't very fit.
  B can swim quickly.
  C likes playing individual sports.

Portfolio 4

Write a report for a school website about a sport that you like playing. Write two paragraphs.

1 **Introduction**
  • What is the sport?
  • Where and when do you play?

2 **Information about the sport**
  • What do players do in this sport?
  • Is it easy/difficult?
  • What are you good at?
  • Does it help you to get fit?

Quiz 4

a What do you remember about Unit 4? Answer all the questions you can and then check in the Student's Book.

A

1 When you ride a bike, what is the name of your sport?

....

2 What sports can you see in picture A?

....

....

B

C

3 Which sport uses the ball in picture B?

....

7 What is the person doing in picture C?

....

4 There are two mistakes in this sentence. Write the correct sentence.

I do skiing and I play athletics.

....

8 What are the adverbs for these adjectives?

quiet .... happy ....

good ....

5 Tick (✓) the correct sentence.

A Eva enjoys to play basketball. ☐

B Eva is enjoying play basketball. ☐

C Eva enjoys playing basketball. ☐

9 Put the words in the correct order.

like / sister / early / My / doesn't / up / getting

....

....

6 Do cricket players kick the ball?

....

10 (Circle) the word that is not an adverb.

lovely   badly   quietly   fast

b 🔊 27 Listen and check.

c Now look at your Student's Book and write two more quiz questions for Unit 4.

Question: ....

....

Answer: ....

Question: ....

....

Answer: ....

5 Fame!

1 Vocabulary

Describing people

a Complete the sentences with adjectives.

Diana

Amir

Craig

Kelly

1 Kelly's got c_url_y... hair.

2 Amir's got s.......................... black hair.

3 Craig's got w.......................... brown hair.

4 Diana's got l.......................... s.......................... hair.

b Write the name of a famous person for each description.

1 .... is short.

2 .... has got blue eyes.

3 .... has got curly hair.

4 .... is slim.

5 .... has got straight hair.

6 .... is very tall.

c Complete the sentences with 's or 's got.
Then draw a picture of Mike.

> My friend Mike ¹.................... tall and he
> ².................... big brown eyes. He ³....................
> quite slim. He ⁴.................... curly blond hair
> and it ⁵.................... very short at the moment.

2 Grammar Grammar reference: page 90

Past simple: the verb *be*

a Complete the sentences with *was*, *wasn't*, *were* or *weren't*.

1 The disco was fun. There .... lots of people and the music .... really good.

2 We .... at the beach on Saturday because the weather .... very nice. It was cold and cloudy.

3 When Enrico .... young, he .... a singer in a band with some friends, but they .... famous.

4 Charlie Chaplin's films .... very popular in the USA, but he .... American. He .... born in London in 1889.

5 I was really excited before the football match, but it .... very good. I don't think the players .... fit and there .... any goals.

b Make questions from these sentences.

1 Rachel was at school yesterday. _Was Rachel at school yesterday?_
2 The film was good. ....
3 The musicians were Australian. ....
4 You were late. Why _were you late?_ ....
5 George was at the sports centre. When ....
6 They weren't born in Portugal. Where ....

(3) Vocabulary

Jobs

a Add vowels (*a, e, i, o, u*) to make words for jobs.

~~wrtr~~	dncr	mdl	ctr	sngr	mscn	rtst	phtgrphr	sprts prsn	bsnss prsn

1 _writer_ .... 5 .... 9 ....
2 .... 6 .... 10 ....
3 .... 7 ....
4 .... 8 ....

b Look at the photos and write sentences. Use words in Exercise 3a.

1 _Anna Pavlova was a dancer._ ....
2 ....
3 ....
4 ....
5 ....
6 ....

> **Check it out!**
>
> We normally use *a/an* when we describe someone's job.
>
> *Shakespeare was **a** writer.*
> *Charlie Chaplin was **an** actor.*

1 Anna Pavlova

2 Jimi Hendrix

3 Greta Garbo

4 Luciano Pavarotti

5 Salvador Dalí

6 Jean Shrimpton

Help yourself!

Nouns ending in -er

We often add -(e)r to a verb to make the noun for a person.

Verb	Noun for a person
sing	a singer
work	a worker
dance	a dancer

Write the nouns for these people.

1 A .... teaches students.

2 A .... drives a bus, taxi, etc.

3 A .... cleans rooms.

4 A .... paints pictures.

5 A .... rides a horse.

6 A .... plays a sport or game.

Write down these words and add others.

---

4 Grammar Grammar reference: page 90

Past simple: regular verbs

a Complete the sentences with these verbs in the past simple.

> listen   start   travel   talk   visit   stay   ~~perform~~

1 Matt and Jenny ..performed.. well in the dance competition.

2 I .... to Janet on the phone last night.

3 It was sunny in the morning, but it ....
to rain in the afternoon.

4 We .... at home and ....
to music.

5 Alex .... to Milan and ....
his Italian penfriend.

b Write sentences with the negative form of the past simple.

1 My sister played the guitar.
(not / the violin)
.She didn't play the violin....................................

2 They moved to Switzerland.
(not / to Italy)
....

3 I wanted an ice cream.
(not / a sandwich)
....

4 We watched a sports programme.
(not / a film)
....

---

5 Our grandparents lived in England.
(not / in the USA)
....

6 He studied Spanish at school.
(not / German)
....

c 🔊 28 Complete the text with these verbs in the past simple. Then listen and check.

> decide   start   move   enjoy   be
> not win   not want

Adriana Lima [1]............................ born in Salvador, Brazil in 1981. At first, she [2]............................ to be a model – she was a quiet child and she [3]............................ reading and taking photos. But in 1994, she [4]............................ to enter a modelling competition in Brazil. Two years later, she was in the Supermodel of the World competition. She [5]............................ , but she was second and lots of people noticed her. She [6]............................ to New York and [7]............................ work as a professional model. The rest is history. Adriana is now one of the world's top models and she earns more than $6 million a year.

5 Listen

a 🔊 **29** Listen to the radio quiz. How many questions does Tom answer correctly? ....

b 🔊 **29** Listen again. Match the two parts of the sentences.

1	☐ Yuri Gagarin	**A**	worked as a model.
2	☐ Marie Curie	**B**	played for Brazil.
3	☐ The Beatles	**C**	travelled in space.
4	☐ Marilyn Monroe	**D**	was Polish.
5	☐ Pelé	**E**	lived in Liverpool.

c 🔊 **30** Listen to three more quiz questions. Can you answer them?

1 ....

2 ....

3 ....

6 Pronunciation

Regular past simple endings: /t/, /d/, /ɪd/

a 🔊 **31** Listen and tick (✓) the correct ending.

	/t/	/d/	/ɪd/		/t/	/d/	/ɪd/
kicked	✓	☐	☐	hated	☐	☐	☐
wanted	☐	☐	☐	talked	☐	☐	☐
started	☐	☐	☐	moved	☐	☐	☐
changed	☐	☐	☐	designed	☐	☐	☐
enjoyed	☐	☐	☐	acted	☐	☐	☐

b 🔊 **31** Listen again and write the words in the correct list.

● kicked ....

●● enjoyed ....

●● wanted ....

c 🔊 **32** Listen and practise saying these sentences.

We watched a film.

He kicked the ball.

They designed a web page.

We wanted a pizza.

I decided to leave.

Practise saying these words

🔊 **33** actor   age
businessman   child   colour
move   musician   perform
photographer   violin
yesterday   young

a Read the profile of Johnny Depp and answer the questions.

MOVIE PROFILES: JOHNNY DEPP

American actor Johnny Depp was born in Kentucky in 1963. He learned to play the guitar and decided to leave school when he was 16 because he wanted to be a musician. His rock band, called The Kids, performed in clubs, but they didn't get a lot of work. So Johnny started working as an actor. His first film was *A Nightmare on Elm Street* in 1984.

Fame arrived three years later with the role of a young policeman in the TV programme *21 Jump Street*. The programme was very popular with teenagers and Johnny was a big star. But he wasn't happy and decided not to continue. After *Jump Street* ended in 1990, he looked for interesting and unusual roles. He starred in many films, such as *Charlie and the Chocolate Factory* and *Sweeney Todd*. His most popular role was Jack Sparrow in the *Pirates of the Caribbean* films.

Today Johnny Depp is world-famous, but he doesn't want the life of a typical Hollywood star. He lives quietly in France and he isn't very friendly to photographers. 'I hate fame,' he says. 'I've done everything I can to avoid it.'

1 Why did Johnny Depp leave school?

....

....

2 When did he first act in a film?

....

3 Why was he famous in the late 1980s?

....

....

4 When did his television job end?

....

5 Who was he in *Pirates of the Caribbean*?

....

6 Where does he live now?

....

Portfolio 5

Write a profile of a member of your family. Before you start, interview the person and find out about:

- where he/she was born
- when he/she was born
- his/her school life
- where he/she worked
- what he/she does now

b What films with Johnny Depp do you know? Do you think he is a good actor? Prepare to talk about this in your next class. Make notes to help you.

....

....

....

....

Quiz 5

a What do you remember about Unit 5? Answer all the questions you can and then check in the Student's Book.

1 There are three famous people in picture A. Who are they?

face: _____

eyes: _____

hair: _____

2 What are the opposites of these adjectives?

tall _____

curly _____

3 (Circle) the word that is different.

blonde   slim   black   wavy

4 Who is the person in photo B and what is her job?

_____

_____

5 Can you find two jobs in this puzzle?

d m a o n d c e e l r

_____   _____

6 What is the difference between an actor and an actress?

_____

_____

7 Which sentence is true about the person in picture C?

A He played football for his father's team. ☐

B He started to write books when he was 15. ☐

C He was born in Spain in July 1981. ☐

8 Write the past simple form of these verbs.

act _____   move _____

study _____

9 Which verbs end with the sound /ɪd/?

worked   started   listened   cooked   wanted

_____

10 Who was the star of the *Twilight* films and *Harry Potter and the Goblet of Fire*?

_____

b 🔊 34 Listen and check.

c Now look at your Student's Book and write two more quiz questions for Unit 5.

Question: _____

_____

Answer: _____

Question: _____

_____

Answer: _____

6 The natural world

1 Grammar

Grammar reference: page 90

Past simple: irregular verbs

a Complete the table.

Verb	Past simple
1 go	went
2 sleep	
3	took
4 come	
5 think	
6	knew
7	said
8 begin	
9 see	
10 get	

b Complete the text with the verbs in the past simple.

Last night I ¹................................ (meet) Annie at 7:30 and we ²................................ (go) to the cinema. The film ³................................ (begin) at 8:00. We ⁴................................ (not have) time to walk to the cinema, so we ⁵................................ (take) the bus. The film was good, and when we ⁶................................ (come) out we ⁷................................ (see) Tony in the café. He and Annie ⁸................................ (have) a pizza, but I ⁹................................ (not be) hungry so I ¹⁰................................ (not eat) anything.

c Look at the pictures and correct the sentences.

1 Adam went out at 8:00. (get up)

He didn't go out. He got up.

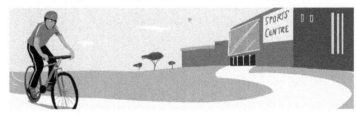

2 He took the bus to the sports centre. (ride)

....

....

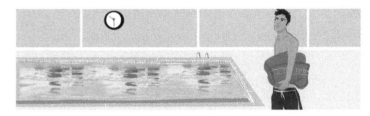

3 His swimming lesson finished at 10:30. (begin)

....

....

4 Jane saw him at the swimming pool. (meet)

....

....

5 They had lunch together. (go)

....

....

② Vocabulary

The natural world

a Find nine more words for things in the natural world in the puzzle.

A	M	I	S	L	A	N	D	L
F	R	O	C	A	D	I	S	A
O	P	S	U	H	I	L	L	K
R	L	E	J	N	W	B	O	E
E	I	A	T	U	T	E	D	T
S	A	V	I	L	L	A	G	E
T	F	I	E	L	D	C	I	B
O	Y	C	N	R	E	H	A	N

b Write words in Exercise 2a under the pictures.

1 ....

2 ....

3 ....

4 ....

5 ....

6 ....

7 ....

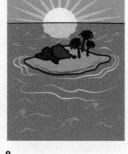

8 ....

c Write an example for each type of place.

1 beach

.Miami..........................

2 river

....

3 island

....

4 lake

....

5 mountain

....

6 village

....

Animals

d Put the boxes in order and make ten words for animals.

in co   r dolp   use p   hin tu

engu   og mo   rd bea   der bi

rtle   w spi   ey fr   ~~monk~~

1 .monkey...........   6 ....
2 .fr...........   7 ....
3 ....   8 ....
4 ....   9 ....
5 ....   10 ....

e Complete the sentences. Use words in Exercise 2d in the singular or plural.

> **Check it out!**
>
> The plural of *mouse* is *mice*.
> *There's a mouse in my room!*
> *Mice are small animals.*

1 A .... is a bird, but it can't fly.

2 .... live in the sea.

3 A .... moves very slowly on land.

4 We get milk from a ....

5 .... have got eight legs.

6 A .... has got long back legs. It can live in water or on land.

7 .... usually live in trees in the forest or the jungle.

8 .... are grey, brown or white. These small animals can run very fast.

③ Read

a Read the text. Are sentences 1–7 right (✓) or wrong (✗)?

In December 2004, big waves from a tsunami in Asia travelled across the sea to Africa. In Kenya, a family of hippos were near the beach when the waves came. Nobody knows what happened to the older animals, but the next day people saw a baby hippo all alone. They took him to Haller Park, an animal park near Mombasa.

When he arrived, the little hippo was tired, lost and terribly unhappy. The workers at Haller called him Owen. They put him together with Mzee, a 130-year-old tortoise – and a strange friendship began.

At first, the tortoise was unfriendly and didn't want the hippo near him. But this soon changed. Mzee seemed to understand that Owen needed him. He showed him where to sleep and what to eat. The two animals went for walks together, swam together and shared the same food. They even had a kind of

'language' that they could both understand. Owen slept next to Mzee, often with his head on the tortoise's front leg.

People began to hear about these animals and thousands of visitors came to see them. Everyone loved the story of the amazing friendship which probably saved the baby hippo's life.

1 The family of hippos lived in Asia. ☐

2 The older animals left the beach before the water arrived. ☐

3 People took Owen to Haller Park because they wanted to help him. ☐

4 Owen and Mzee were both very young animals. ☐

5 At first Mzee didn't want to make friends with Owen. ☐

6 Later the two animals walked, went swimming, ate and slept together. ☐

7 Lots of people visited Haller Park. ☐

b Can you find more information about Owen and Mzee? Look on the internet. Write notes.

----

④ Grammar Grammar reference: page 90

Past simple: questions and short answers

a 🔊 35 Complete the questions with *did*, *was* or *were*. Then listen and check.

1 A: ..Did.. you go to the beach on Sunday?
   B: Yes, we did.

2 A: .... it cold in the mountains?
   B: Yes, it was.

3 A: .... Eva take these photos?
   B: No, I took them.

4 A: Where .... you see the spider?
   B: In my room.

> **Check it out!**
>
> Remember, we never use *do* or *did* in questions with the verb *be*.
>
> *Was Kim at the party?*
> *When were you in Canada?*

5 A: What .... Jack say to you?
   B: Nothing. I didn't speak to him.

6 A: Where .... you last night?
   B: I was at the cinema.

7 A: When .... your parents get home?
   B: At midnight.

b There are mistakes in these questions. ~~Cross out~~ the wrong word(s) and write the correct word(s).

1 ~~Simon told~~ you about the party?

  Did Simon tell ....

2 Which film you saw last night?

  ....

3 Did you ate all the chocolates?

  ....

4 Where your friends were yesterday?

  ....

5 When did the concert began?

  ....

6 Why they were late?

  ....

c Look at the picture. Write past simple questions and then answer them.

1 Where / Helen / go / yesterday?

  Where did Helen go yesterday? ....

  She went to Lion Island. ....

2 she / go / alone?

  ....

  ....

3 What / be / the weather like?

  ....

  ....

4 How / she / get / to the island?

  ....

  ....

5 What / she / take / with her?

  ....

  ....

6 What / she / see / in the water?

  ....

  ....

d Write your own questions for these answers.

1 ....

  Yes, I did.

2 ....

  No, I didn't.

3 ....

  Two days ago.

4 ....

  Last weekend.

5 ....

  Yes, it was.

6 ....

  I was at school.

Help yourself!

last and **ago**

Look at these examples: *I saw a good film **last week**.*   *I met Patrice **two years ago**.*

Then write the words/phrases in the correct table.

weekend	three weeks	July	month	a month	six months	year	a year	100 years

last	_week_		ago
	....	....	
	....	....	
	....	....	

(5) Pronunciation

was and *were*: strong and weak forms

a 🔊 **36** Listen and <u>underline</u> the main stress.

Was he tired?   Were you hot?   Was it boring?
Were they friendly?

b 🔊 **37** Listen and repeat.

Was it rainy? Yes, it was.
Was it sunny? No, it wasn't.
Were you cold? Yes, we were.
Were you happy? No, we weren't!

c 🔊 **38** Listen and practise saying the chant.

> **Practise saying these words**
>
> 🔊 **39** beach   bear   field
> hungry   island   jungle   month
> shake   strange   swam   tortoise
> village

(6) Listen

🔊 **40** Listen to Julie talking about her weekend. Choose the correct answer: A, B or C.

1 Last weekend Julie went away with
  A Scott.
  B Louise.
  C her family.

2 They went on
  A Friday.
  B Saturday.
  C Sunday.

3 They stayed in a village
  A by the sea.
  B on a hill.
  C near a lake.

4 On Saturday morning Julie
  A swam in the lake.
  B rode a horse.
  C went in a boat.

5 She saw lots of
  A horses.
  B tourists.
  C birds.

Portfolio 6

Think about the last six months and write two paragraphs.

Paragraph 1: Describe one good thing that happened.
Paragraph 2: Describe one bad thing that happened.

- Start each paragraph with a time expression:

In August …
Last June/Tuesday …
Last month/week …
Three months/weeks/days ago …

- Write three (or more) sentences in each paragraph.
- Use verbs in the past simple.
- Remember, you can sometimes use *and*, *but* or *because*.

Quiz 6

a What do you remember about Unit 6? Answer all the questions you can and then check in the Student's Book.

A

B

C

1 In April 2010, where were the girls in picture A? Name the country.

....

2 What is the past simple of these verbs?

come ....

say ....

make ....

3 Circle the verb that is different.

swam   saw   play   ate

4 Correct this question.

Where you went last Friday?

....

5 Write the question and answer in the past simple.

A: What do you do when you get home?

B: I have something to eat and I begin my homework.

....

....

....

6 Which sentence is true? Tick (✓) the correct sentence.

A The Andes are mountains in South America. ☐

B The Andes is a river in Asia. ☐

C The Andes are islands in the Caribbean. ☐

7 Circle the words that can complete this sentence: We swam in the ...

lake   hill   river   field   beach   sea

8 There are three animals in picture B. What are they?

....

....

9 Which animals don't live in the jungle?

monkeys   spiders   frogs   cows

....

10 What are the animals in picture C?

....

b 🔊 41 Listen and check.

c Now look at your Student's Book and write two more quiz questions for Unit 6.

Question: ....

....

Answer: ....

Question: ....

....

Answer: ....

7 Mealtime

1 Vocabulary
Food and drink

a Complete the crossword. Use the clues to help you.

b Complete the sentences.

1 A drink that you make with fruit is called
   j.uice.. .
2 T........................ is a type of food we get
   from fish.
3 A c........................ is an orange-coloured
   vegetable.
4 A s........................ is a small red fruit.
5 Spaghetti and lasagne are types of
   p........................ .
6 A b........................ is a yellow fruit. It
   comes from warm countries.
7 M........................ is white and it comes
   from cows.
8 An o........................ is a vegetable that is
   usually white or brown.

2 Grammar Grammar reference: page 92
a/an, some and any

> **Check it out!**
>
> Remember, uncountable nouns are
> always singular. There is no plural form.

a Complete the table with your answers from
Exercise 1b.

Countable nouns	Uncountable nouns
....	juice........................
....	....
....	....
....	....

b Write C (countable noun) or U (uncountable
noun).

1 lemon ....   6 bird ....
2 ham ....   7 photo ....
3 meat ....   8 money ....
4 vegetable ....   9 music ....
5 rice ....   10 village ....

c What can you see in the picture? Use *a*, *an* or *some*.

I can see .... ,

.... ,

.... ,

.... ,

....

and ....

d Complete the sentences with *some* or *any*.

1 I want to buy .... strawberries.

2 Are there .... eggs in these biscuits?

3 There's .... tuna in the cupboard.

4 I bought .... nice red apples this morning.

5 Have we got .... bread?

6 There weren't .... grapes at the supermarket.

7 The dog wants .... water.

8 We don't need .... cheese for this recipe.

3 Listen

a 🔊 42 Listen to the conversation. Where is the man going?

....

b 🔊 42 Listen again and complete the shopping list.

Shopping list
1 .... juice
milk
six 2 ....
3 ....
tuna

Fruit & vegetables
new 4 ....
carrots
5 ....
two 6 ....

4 Grammar Grammar reference: page 92

a lot of, *much* and *many*

a Match the two parts of the sentences.

1	How much	A food at the party?
2	There's a lot	B onions.
3	There aren't many	C orange juice.
4	How many	D of tomatoes in this salad.
5	We haven't got much	E milk have we got?
6	Was there much	F strawberries in the garden?
7	There are a lot	G of ham on this pizza.
8	Are there many	H potatoes do you want?

b Complete the sentences with *much* or *many*.

1 Have you got .... homework this weekend?

2 How .... subjects is Ali studying this year?

3 Quick! We haven't got .... time.

4 Was there .... snow here last winter?

5 Did they take .... photos in Thailand?

6 How .... money have you got?

7 There weren't .... people at the party.

c 🔊 **43** Read the conversation and choose the correct answer: A, B or C. Then listen and check.

Greg:	I'm really hungry. What did you have for lunch?
Robbie:	Nothing! I wanted to make ¹...... sandwich, but we haven't got ²...... bread.
Greg:	OK, we can have ³...... pasta. Is there ⁴...... olive oil?
Robbie:	Yes, and we've got ⁵...... tomatoes.
Greg:	Good. I can use them for the sauce. I want ⁶...... onion too.
Robbie:	How ⁷...... water do we need for the pasta?
Greg:	Quite a lot. And don't forget to add ⁸...... salt.

1	**A** a	**B** some	**C** a lot of
2	**A** a	**B** any	**C** many
3	**A** some	**B** much	**C** many
4	**A** an	**B** many	**C** any
5	**A** much	**B** many	**C** a lot of
6	**A** a	**B** an	**C** any
7	**A** lot of	**B** much	**C** many
8	**A** a	**B** much	**C** some

⑤ Vocabulary

Food collocations

a Tick (✓) two correct answers for each question.

1 What can you eat with steak?

bananas ☐   tuna ☐   salad ☐   potatoes ☐

2 What can you use to make fruit juice?

onions ☐   apples ☐   oranges ☐   fish ☐

3 What can you put on a pizza?

ham ☐   rice ☐   cheese ☐   bread ☐

4 What can you use to make soup?

potatoes ☐   grapes ☐   strawberries ☐   carrots ☐

5 What can you put in a salad?

lemonade ☐   eggs ☐   tomatoes ☐   biscuits ☐

6 What type of ice cream can you buy?

vanilla ☐   chocolate ☐   pepper ☐   bacon ☐

b (Circle) the correct words.

1 I'd like some *strawberry / strawberries* ice cream, please.
2 I'm making some *potato / tomato* sauce for the pasta for lunch.
3 They've got *apple / chicken* soup on the menu at the café today.
4 I love chocolate *biscuits / sandwiches*.
5 Have we got a lemon? I'd like some lemon *juice / salad* on my fish.

c How often do you eat these things? Tick (✓) the box.

	often	sometimes	never
vegetable soup	☐	☐	☐
vanilla ice cream	☐	☐	☐
a ham sandwich	☐	☐	☐
apple juice	☐	☐	☐
a cheeseburger	☐	☐	☐

Help yourself!

Countable or uncountable

Sometimes a noun can be countable or uncountable.

*We need to buy **some coffee**.*
(= uncountable)

*Would you like **a coffee**?*
(= a cup of coffee, countable)

*I bought **some chicken**.*
(= type of meat, uncountable)

*I bought **a chicken**.*
(= a whole bird, countable)

Write *C* (countable) or *U* (uncountable) for the underlined nouns in these sentences.

1 There's some <u>tomato juice</u> in the fridge.

....

2 Can I have a <u>tomato juice</u>, please?

....

3 You need some <u>steak</u> for this recipe.

....

4 I'd like a <u>steak</u>, please.

....

If you are not sure how to use a noun, look at the example sentences in your English dictionary.

(6) Pronunciation

/e/ and /æ/

a 🔊 44 Listen and (circle) the word you hear.

bad	bed
sad	said
had	head
man	men
band	bend
mat	met

b 🔊 45 Listen and repeat the word pairs.

c 🔊 46 Listen to the poem.

MATTIE

I travelled to Paris,
I went to Japan,
Played tennis in Venice
And sang in a band,
But I was unhappy
And that didn't end
Until I met Mattie,
My fabulous friend.

d 🔊 47 Listen and practise saying each line of the poem.

e Practise saying the whole poem.

Practise saying these words

🔊 48 biscuit   cheese   chocolate
juice   money   onion   orange
potato   recipe   sauce   steak
yoghurt

7 Read

Read the food facts and answer the questions.

DID YOU KNOW ...?

- The tomato isn't a vegetable – it's a fruit.

- The word *tomato* is Mexican, but the first tomatoes were probably from Peru. The Spanish took them to Europe in the 1500s.

- Today about 25% of the world's tomatoes come from China.

- The first carrots were purple, red or black. Our orange carrots come from a type that people produced in the 1500s in Holland.

- Potatoes and tomatoes are from the same family.

- The first potatoes came from the Andes. Europeans didn't eat many potatoes until the 1700s.

- Chips are often called *French fries* – but people probably began making them in Belgium, not France.

- There are over 40,000 different types of rice in the world.

- Today rice is the main food for over half the world's people. In some Asian languages the word for *rice* also means *food*.

- In Burma, a person eats about 225 kilos of rice every year – half a kilo every day.

- One type of banana, called the *ice-cream banana*, is blue when the fruit is young. It turns yellow when it is ready to eat.

- Another type of banana is brown or purple, and the fruit inside is slightly pink.

---

1 Where does the word *tomato* come from?

....

2 Correct the information in this sentence: *The tomato is a vegetable which first arrived in Europe in the 1500s.*

....

3 What was unusual about Dutch carrots in the 1500s?

....

4 When did potatoes start to be popular in Europe?

....

5 How many people in the world eat rice as their main food?

....

6 How much rice does a Burmese person eat in a day?

....

7 Tick (✓) the correct sentence.

   a Ice-cream bananas aren't ready to eat when they are blue. ☐

   b People eat ice cream with blue bananas. ☐

   c Ice-cream bananas are pink inside. ☐

Portfolio 7

Make a poster about the things you eat and drink. Write three paragraphs with these headings:

1 Breakfast

2 Lunch

3 Dinner

Here are some expressions you can use:

I often/usually/always have …
I like/love …
I don't like / I hate …
I eat/drink a lot of …
I don't eat much/many …

Add pictures or photos to your poster.

Quiz 7

a What do you remember about Unit 7? Answer all the questions you can and then check in the Student's Book.

1 (Circle) the two uncountable nouns.

biscuit   milk   carrot   olive   cheese

6 Look at the person in picture A. What type of books does he write?

....

2 The name and the colour of this fruit are the same. What is it?

....

7 Use these words/phrases to make four food collocations.

ham   ice cream   fruit   soup   vanilla   sandwich vegetable   juice

....

....

3 (Circle) the word that's different.

onion   potato   lemon   carrot

8 What is picture B?

....

....

4 Find two kinds of meat in this puzzle. Write the words.

    k a e t s n e k c i h c

....

9 You are in a café. Ask for the food and drink in the picture.

Can ....

....

....

5 There are two mistakes in this sentence. Write the correct sentence.

We've got many bananas, but we haven't got much grapes.

....

....

....

10 (Circle) the two words with the /æ/ sound.

banana   carrot   sauce   salt lemonade   salad   potato

b 🔊 49 Listen and check.

c Now look at your Student's Book and write two more quiz questions for Unit 7.

Question: ....

....

Answer: ....

Question: ....

....

Answer: ....

8 At home

1 Vocabulary

Parts of a house

a Put the letters in the correct order and write the words in the puzzle. Then use the eight ⬡ letters to make one more word for a place in the house.

1 VILGIN MORO

2 HKCINTE

3 DEOMOBR

4 GINNID OROM

5 DRANGE

6 LHAL

7 RITSAS

b Complete the sentences with the words in Exercise 1a.

1 A .... is a room for sleeping.

2 A .... is a room for cooking food.

3 A .... always has a table and chairs.

4 People sit, talk, watch TV and listen to music in the ....

5 You see trees and flowers in a ....

6 People wash in the ....

7 You can go up and down the ....

8 People often put their coats and umbrellas in the ....

2 Grammar Grammar reference: page 94

Comparative adjectives

a Match the two parts of the sentences.

1 ☐ A flat is usually cheaper   **A** than horses.

2 ☐ Spain is a warmer country   **B** than Geography.

3 ☐ A car is more expensive   **C** than a house.

4 ☐ The weather was worse yesterday   **D** than a bicycle.

   E than yesterday.

5 ☐ Elephants are heavier   **F** than today.

6 ☐ I think History is more interesting   **G** than Scotland.

7 ☐ It's sunnier today

Help yourself!

Compound nouns (2)

Bedroom and *bathroom* are two more examples of compound nouns.

Look at the nouns with *house* and *chair* and match them with the pictures. Use your dictionary if you need to.

greenhouse ☐   · boathouse ☐

lighthouse ☐   wheelchair ☐

deckchair ☐   armchair ☐

 1   2   3

 4   5    6

In compound nouns, the main stress is on the first word:

<u>green</u>house   <u>wheel</u>chair.

Dictionaries put a small line before the stressed part of the word:

ˈgriːnhaʊs   ˈwiːltʃeə

Use your dictionary to check the stress in English words.

Check it out!

Spelling of -er adjectives

Adjectives ending in a consonant + -*y*: change to -*ier*.

easy → easier   happy → happier

Adjectives ending in one vowel + a consonant: double the consonant + -*er*.

*big → bi**gg**er   sad → sa**dd**er*

b Complete the sentences with comparative adjectives and *than*.

1 Tarik is .... (tall) his father.

2 Pop stars are .... (famous) writers.

3 My sister is .... (pretty) me.

4 The living room is .... (big) the dining room.

5 The film was .... (good) the book.

6 The Maths exam was .... (difficult) the Science one.

c Write sentences with the comparative form of these adjectives.

| modern | noisy | ~~young~~ | far | slim | expensive |

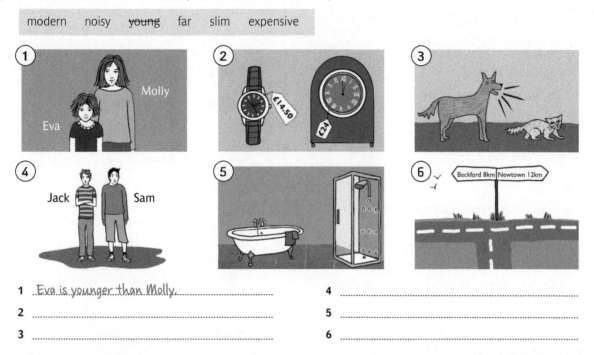

1 _Eva is younger than Molly._

2 ....

3 ....

4 ....

5 ....

6 ....

③ Vocabulary

Furniture and objects

a Look at the pictures. Complete the puzzle and find the mystery word.

b ~~Cross out~~ the wrong word in each sentence. Write the correct word.

1 I often wash my hair when I have a ~~desk~~. ....shower..................

2 We cook our food on the sofa. ....

3 I sleep in a cupboard. ....

4 People put their computer on a rug or a table. ....

5 Food stays cool in the bath. ....

6 A shower is a big cupboard for clothes. ....

(4) Grammar Grammar reference: page 94

Superlative adjectives

a (Circle) the correct words.

1 I'm the *shortest / shorter / most short* person in my family.

2 July is usually *hottest / the hottest / most hottest* month of the year in Europe.

3 Today was the *happier / happiest / most happy* day of my life.

4 Dad always sits in *more comfortable / most comfortable / the most comfortable* chair.

5 I think Monday is the *worst / worse / badly* day of the week.

6 The Beatles were the world's *popular / more popular / most popular* band in the 1960s.

> **Check it out!**
>
> **Spelling of -est adjectives**
> Follow the rules for *-er* adjectives.
> *easy → easier → easiest*
> *happy → happier → happiest*
>
> *big → bigger → biggest*
> *sad → sadder → saddest*

b 🔊 50 Find the correct picture and complete each sentence with a superlative adjective. Then listen and check.

8,850 metres

320 km per hour

28 cm

5,000 kg

3,692 km

−54°C

1 Everest is the .... mountain in the world.

2 The Volga is the .... river in Europe.

3 The world's .... land animal is the African elephant.

4 The .... place in the world is Antarctica.

5 Goliath bird-eating tarantulas are the .... spiders in the world.

6 The .... bird is the peregrine falcon.

c Complete the sentences with your opinions. Use five of these adjectives in the superlative form.

> big good bad interesting popular funny noisy easy

1 .... is .... programme on TV.
2 .... is .... person in my family.
3 .... is .... subject for me this year.
4 .... is .... city in my country.
5 .... is .... song at the moment.

5 Pronunciation

The schwa /ə/ in comparatives and superlatives

a 🔊 51 Listen and (circle) the /ə/ sounds.

Dad is older than Mum.
Portugal is warmer than England.
The house was nicer than the flat.

The singers were better than the dancers.
Russia is the biggest country in the world.
Janet was the tallest person in the team.

b 🔊 51 Listen again and repeat the sentences.

> **Practise saying these words**
> 🔊 52 autumn bathroom beautiful comfortable cupboard
> fridge hall pretty roof traditional wardrobe worse

6 Listen

🔊 53 Listen to the conversations. Choose the correct answer: A, B or C.

1 Where is the coffee?

  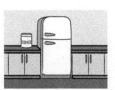

A ☐ B ☐ C ☐

2 Which is Tom's bedroom?

A ☐ B ☐ C ☐

3 Which is the best phone for Cathy?

A ☐ Maxitone B ☐ Carlton C ☐ Primo

4 Which is the bathroom door in Rosa's house?

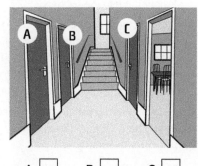

A ☐ B ☐ C ☐

5 Which girl is Sophie?

A ☐ B ☐ C ☐

(7) Read

a Read Alice's email to her cousin. Then look at the plan and name the parts of the flat (1–7).

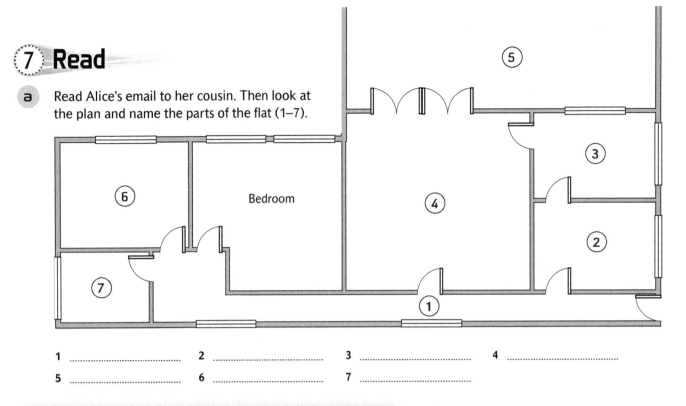

Bedroom

1 .... 2 .... 3 .... 4 ....

5 .... 6 .... 7 ....

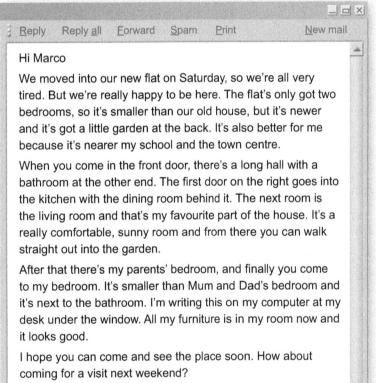

Reply   Reply all   Forward   Spam   Print   New mail

Hi Marco

We moved into our new flat on Saturday, so we're all very tired. But we're really happy to be here. The flat's only got two bedrooms, so it's smaller than our old house, but it's newer and it's got a little garden at the back. It's also better for me because it's nearer my school and the town centre.

When you come in the front door, there's a long hall with a bathroom at the other end. The first door on the right goes into the kitchen with the dining room behind it. The next room is the living room and that's my favourite part of the house. It's a really comfortable, sunny room and from there you can walk straight out into the garden.

After that there's my parents' bedroom, and finally you come to my bedroom. It's smaller than Mum and Dad's bedroom and it's next to the bathroom. I'm writing this on my computer at my desk under the window. All my furniture is in my room now and it looks good.

I hope you can come and see the place soon. How about coming for a visit next weekend?

Love
Alice

b Are the sentences *right* (✓) or *wrong* (✗) or *doesn't say* (–)?

1 The flat is more modern than the house.

2 The flat is further from Alice's school than the house.

3 Alice walks to school.

4 Alice thinks the living room is the worst room in the flat.

5 She's got a smaller bedroom than her parents.

6 There's a bath in the flat.

Portfolio 8

Compare your bedroom with the one in the picture. How are they different? Write a description.

Here are some expressions you can use:

My room / The room in the picture
    is / has got …
I've got …   There's / There are …
The furniture is …
I think …   I (don't) like …

Use some of these adjectives in the comparative form.

big   small   good   bad   nice
modern   comfortable   clean
pretty   interesting   boring

Quiz (8)

a **a** What do you remember about Unit 8? Answer all the questions you can and then check in the Student's Book.

1 Name the room where you can have a shower.

....

2 What rooms can you see in picture A?

....

....

3 They go up and down inside a house, but they never move. What are they?

....

4 (Circle) the word that is different.

sofa   fridge   cupboard   cooker

5 Where is the house in picture B? Name the country.

....

6 What is the comparative form of these adjectives?

easy ....

good ....

expensive ....

7 What is the superlative form of these adjectives?

long ....   far ....

interesting ....

8 There are two mistakes in this sentence. Write the correct sentence.

Canada is more big than the USA, but Russia is the bigger country in the world.

....

....

....

9 What is the opposite of *best*?

....

10 In picture C, 1 is at the top and 2 is on the left. Where are 3 and 4?

....

....

b 🔊 54 Listen and check.

c Now look at your Student's Book and write two more quiz questions for Unit 8.

Question: ....

....

Answer: ....

Question: ....

....

Answer: ....

9 Go to town

1 Grammar

Grammar reference: page 86

Present continuous for future plans

a Look at the <u>underlined</u> words in the phone conversations. Are the people talking about the present or the future? Write *P* (present) or *F* (future).

> A: Jess, this is Sara. Where are you? ¹<u>We're waiting</u> for you.
>
> B: ²<u>I'm coming</u>! ³<u>I'm walking</u> down King Street now.
>
> A: Well, be quick. ⁴<u>We're leaving</u> in five minutes.

1 ☐ 2 ☐ 3 ☐ 4 ☐

> A: Hey, Simon, ⁵<u>are you doing</u> anything after lunch?
>
> B: Nothing much. Why? ⁶<u>What's happening</u> this afternoon?
>
> A: Well, ⁷<u>Matthew's staying</u> here at the moment and ⁸<u>we're going</u> to the cinema at 3 o'clock. Do you want to come?

5 ☐ 6 ☐ 7 ☐ 8 ☐

b Complete the sentences with the verbs in the present continuous.

have	meet	study	play	stay
arrive	not cook	not go		

1 A: .... Nick and Miguel .... hockey tomorrow?

   B: No, they aren't. They .... for their exams.

2 My aunt .... from Rome on Friday. We .... her at the airport.

3 I .... out with my friends this evening. I .... at home.

4 A: What .... we .... for dinner?

   B: Pizzas. Dad says he .... tonight.

c Look at Harry's diary for next weekend and complete the sentences.

Saturday
12:00	lunch with Greg at the Bluebird Café
3:30	basketball game at Harris Park
8:00	concert with Paul and Ellen

Sunday
8:30–12:30	work at the supermarket
3:00	football match on TV
evening	homework

1 On Saturday afternoon <u>he's playing basketball at Harris Park.</u>

2 On Sunday afternoon ....

3 On Saturday night ....

4 On Sunday evening ....

5 At twelve on Saturday ....

6 On Sunday morning ....

Help yourself!

Future time expressions

Remember these future time expressions:
tomorrow (morning/afternoon/evening/night)
the day after tomorrow
on Monday (morning/afternoon/evening/night)
next weekend/week/month/year

It's 10 o'clock on Wednesday morning. Number these expressions in order, from the soonest (1) to the latest (9).

☐ tomorrow evening   ☐ next week

☐ on Sunday morning   ☐ tonight

☐ tomorrow afternoon   ☐ next year

☐1 this afternoon   ☐ next month

☐ tomorrow morning

(2) Vocabulary

Buildings and places

a Add vowels (*a, e, i, o, u*) to make words for places in town.

| ḙf | sttn | bnk | cr prk | shppng cntr | lbrry | ftbll grnd | msm | pst ffc |

1 café _____   4 _____   7 _____

2 _____   5 _____   8 _____

3 _____   6 _____   9 _____

b Match the words in Exercise 2a with the photos. Write 1–9 in the boxes.

c Write true answers to these questions.

1 Where's your nearest post office?   3 Is there a car park at your school?   5 What's the nearest station to your home?

_____   _____   _____

2 What's your favourite café?   4 Name a museum in your area.

_____   _____

(3) Grammar Grammar reference: page 94

Prepositions of place

a Write the prepositions.

1 The girl is _____ her brother.   2 She's _____ her brother.   3 She's _____ her brother.

4 She's _____ her brother.   5 She's _____ her brother and her father.

b Read the information. Then draw and write the names of the <u>underlined</u> places on the map.

A: Let me draw a map for you. This is Palmer Street. On the left at the bottom of the map there's a <u>car park</u> and the <u>hospital</u> is next to it. The <u>museum</u> is opposite the car park and it's got a small <u>garden</u> in front of it. The <u>post office</u> is next to the museum, and the <u>bank</u> is between the post office and the supermarket. There's a small <u>café</u> behind the bank.

B: OK. I'll meet you at the café after school.

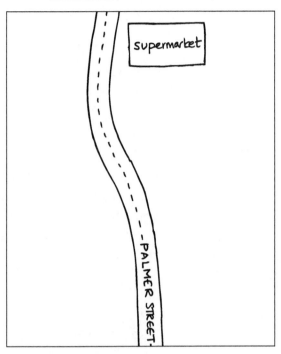

c [🔊] **55** Complete the text. Write one word for each space. Then listen and check.

You can't see our house from here because it's
¹ _behind_ the church. When you walk up
Princes Street, it's ² .... the left, next
³ .... the Black Cat Café.

My room is upstairs ⁴ .... the right.
I've got a desk ⁵ .... front ⁶ ....
the window and I like looking out because our
house is ⁷ .... the park. My desk is
⁸ .... the bed and the wardrobe.

(4) Pronunciation

Linking words

a [🔊] **56** Listen and draw a line between the words that are linked.

1 She's‿at‿a hotel‿in‿Australia.

2 They're opening the shop at eight o'clock.

3 Cook some onions in olive oil.

4 We had our English exam a week ago.

b [🔊] **57** Listen and repeat.

1 in Australia
at a hotel in Australia
She's at a hotel in Australia.

2 at eight o'clock
the shop at eight o'clock
They're opening the shop at eight o'clock.

3 olive oil
onions in olive oil
Cook some onions in olive oil.

4 a week ago
English exam a week ago
We had our English exam a week ago.

Practise saying these words

[🔊] **58** birthday   concert   front   ground
library   local   museum   opposite
orchestra   station   tomorrow   volleyball

5 Vocabulary

Shops

a ~~Cross out~~ the wrong shop in each sentence. Write the correct shop.

1 This ~~bookshop~~ is expensive, but it's got fantastic shoes.   _shoe shop_

2 They went to a supermarket to plan their holiday.   ....

3 Our rabbit Snowy came from the clothes shop in Park Road.   ....

4 You can buy a lot of different magazines at the shoe shop.   ....

5 Mum came home with five bags of food from the chemist's.   ....

6 I bought this dictionary at the travel agent's in West Street.   ....

7 The best place for T-shirts is the newsagent's opposite the bank.   ....

8 People often go to a pet shop after a visit to the doctor.   ....

b Where can you see 1–6? Name the shops.

1 ....

2 ....

3 ....

4 ....

5 ....

6 ....

(1)
Lorenzo
Jacket
Style P803/4
Black Size M

(2)

BISCUITS CHOC CHIP	£0.54
EGGS M X6	£1.36
RICE 500G	£0.89
CHEESE 270G	£2.00
LEMONS 2 @ £0.30	£0.60
CARROTS	£0.87
TOTAL 32 ARTICLES	£82.47

(3)
ISTANBUL
Holiday package
Flight + 7 nights, 3* hotel
from £298

(4) Hart's Quality Fish Food
for all types of tropical and cold water fish

(5) Foreign newspapers

(6) Travel books and maps

6 Listen

a 🔊 59 Listen and write the correct letter.

1 ☐   A station

2 ☐   B library

              C travel agent's

3 ☐   D museum

              E supermarket

4 ☐   F bookshop

5 ☐   G café

b 🔊 59 Listen again and answer the question for each recording.

1 What time is the place closing?

....

2 What does the man want to eat first?

....

3 What city is the train going to?

....

4 What does the woman want to buy?

....

5 Where is the man going next June?

....

(7) Read

Read this page from a school newsletter and answer the questions.

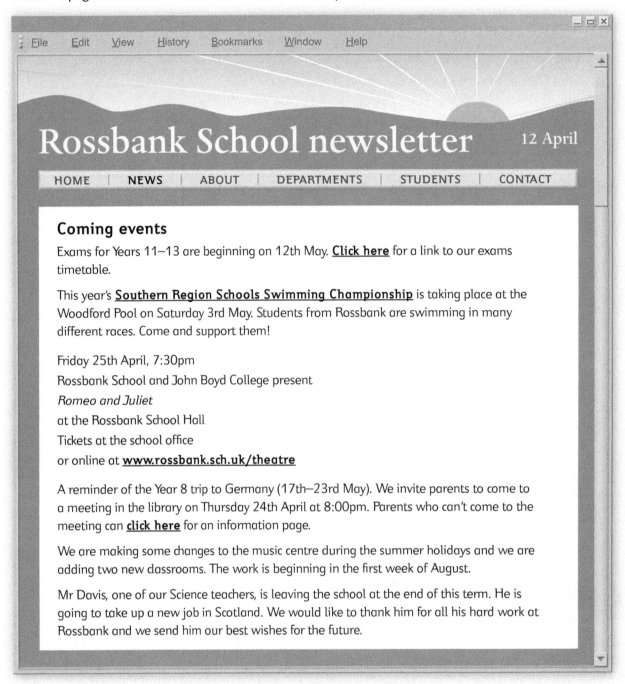

File   Edit   View   History   Bookmarks   Window   Help

Rossbank School newsletter   12 April

| HOME | NEWS | ABOUT | DEPARTMENTS | STUDENTS | CONTACT |

Coming events

Exams for Years 11–13 are beginning on 12th May. **Click here** for a link to our exams timetable.

This year's **Southern Region Schools Swimming Championship** is taking place at the Woodford Pool on Saturday 3rd May. Students from Rossbank are swimming in many different races. Come and support them!

Friday 25th April, 7:30pm
Rossbank School and John Boyd College present
Romeo and Juliet
at the Rossbank School Hall
Tickets at the school office
or online at **www.rossbank.sch.uk/theatre**

A reminder of the Year 8 trip to Germany (17th–23rd May). We invite parents to come to a meeting in the library on Thursday 24th April at 8:00pm. Parents who can't come to the meeting can **click here** for an information page.

We are making some changes to the music centre during the summer holidays and we are adding two new classrooms. The work is beginning in the first week of August.

Mr Davis, one of our Science teachers, is leaving the school at the end of this term. He is going to take up a new job in Scotland. We would like to thank him for all his hard work at Rossbank and we send him our best wishes for the future.

1 Where are some students going in the middle of May?

....

2 When are students acting in a theatre performance?

....

3 When are Year 12 students starting their exams?

....

4 Where is a sports competition happening soon?

....

5 Who is moving to a different part of the UK?

....

6 Which building is changing later in the year?

....

Portfolio 9

Imagine your school is having a sports competition, a concert and a theatre performance next month. Choose <u>one</u> of these events and write an invitation to parents for a school newsletter. Include:

• information about the event
• time and place
• directions to the place

Quiz 9

a What do you remember about Unit 9? Answer all the questions you can and then check in the Student's Book.

1 What is the boy doing in picture A?

....

2 When can we use the present continuous? Tick (✓) the correct answer.
- **A** ☐ to talk about the present only
- **B** ☐ to talk about the present and the past
- **C** ☐ to talk about the present and the future

3 Match the words to make three time expressions.

next   morning
tomorrow   after tomorrow
the day   weekend

....
....
....

4 Write the correct question and answer.
- **A:** You go out on tomorrow night?
- **B:** No, I don't. I stay at home.

....
....

5 What do you think the signs mean in picture B? Name the three places.

1 ....   3 ....

2 ....

6 Match the words to make four places in town.

shopping   shoe   football   travel

ground   agent's   shop   centre

....

....

7 In what shop can you buy sausages, potatoes, coffee, fruit juice and pasta?

....

8 Where is the boy in picture C?

....

9 Complete the directions for picture D.

Go straight .... and .... the .... left. The house is .... the right, ... the cinema.

10 Put the words in the correct order to make an invitation.

Saturday / a / come / on / Would / to / like / to / you / party ?

....
....

b 🔊 60 Listen and check.

c Now look at your Student's Book and write two more quiz questions for Unit 9.

Question: ....
....
Answer: ....

Question: ....
....
Answer: ....

10 Looking good

1 Vocabulary

Clothes

a Put the letters in the correct order and write the words for clothes (1–14).

> stobo   toca   cossk   jektac   hosse   thrisT-   prejmu
> trisk   ussertor   thross   thisgt   ~~serds~~   sinterra   rsith

Check it out!

Remember, some clothes words (for example, *trousers*) are always plural. The word *clothes* is the same – it has no singular form.

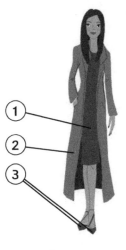 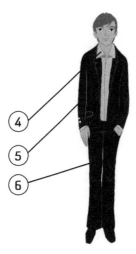 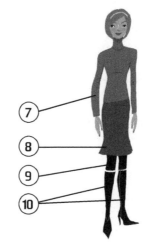 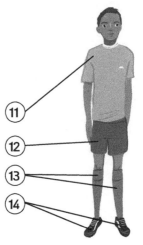

1 _dress_____ 4 _____ 7 _____ 10 _____ 13 _____

2 _____ 5 _____ 8 _____ 11 _____ 14 _____

3 _____ 6 _____ 9 _____ 12 _____

b Write the words for clothes. Choose words in Exercise 1a and use each word only once.

1 You wear these inside your shoes.

   _socks_____

2 These are two types of shoes.

   _____ and _____

3 These two things are women's clothes.

   a _____ and a _____

4 This is a short coat.

   _____

5 These clothes cover your legs.

   _____ and _____

6 Football and tennis players wear them.

   _____

7 These two things keep you warm in the winter.

   a _____ and a _____

8 This is a comfortable top to wear with jeans in hot weather.

   a _____

2 Grammar   Grammar reference: page 98

have to and *don't have to*

a Match the two parts of the sentences.

1 ☐ My brother has

2 ☐ We have to

3 ☐ What time do you have

4 ☐ Anna doesn't have to

5 ☐ Drivers have

6 ☐ How much do we have to

7 ☐ I don't have

A to leave?

B wear her uniform at the weekend.

C to do any homework this evening.

D pay for the tickets?

E wear warm clothes in the winter.

F to study for his exams this weekend.

G to stop at a red light.

b Write sentences with the positive or negative form of *have to*.

1 You can't turn left at Bridge Street.
(You / go straight on)

You have to go straight on.

2 My swimming lesson starts at 8:15.
(I / leave home at 7:45)

----

3 The concert is free.
(We / buy tickets)

----

4 Beth is leaving now.
(She / get to the station before 8:30)

----

5 You've got lots of time.
(You / hurry)

----

6 He isn't sick.
(He / go to the doctor's)

----

7 It's difficult to hear the words of this song.
(You / listen carefully)

----

c Write true answers to these questions.

1 In your country, do people have to go to school when they are 16?

----

2 Do students have to wear a uniform at your school?

----

3 Which subjects do you have to study this year?

----

4 What time do you have to get up on school days?

----

5 What time do you have to be at school?

----

(3) Vocabulary

Accessories

a Look at the table: 4 is A, 6 is C and 8 is R. Write all these letters in the puzzle. Then complete the words for accessories and write the correct letters in the table.

1	2	3	4	5	6	7	8
			A		C		R

9	10	11	12	13	14	15	16

b Complete the sentences with words in Exercise 3a.

1 I'm wearing a .... on my finger.

2 She's wearing a pair of .... in her ears.

3 .... are good for your eyes on sunny days.

4 He's wearing a .... on his head.

5 You can wear a .... with trousers. It goes around the middle of your body.

6 Look at your .... to find the time.

7 I'm wearing a silver .... on my arm.

8 You can wear a .... around your neck on a cold day.

Help yourself!

Plural -ves

Most words ending with -f or -fe have an irregular plural with -ves.

leaf → lea**ves**   knife → kni**ves**

Write the plural form of these nouns.

scarf   ....

life   ....

shelf   ....

wife   ....

half   ....

To find out if a noun has an irregular plural form, look in your dictionary.

(4) Pronunciation

/v/ and /f/

a   🔊 61 Listen to the words and tick (✓) the sound you hear. If you do not hear /v/ or /f/, tick ✗.

	/v/	/f/	✗		/v/	/f/	✗
1	✓	☐	☐	**7**	☐	☐	☐
2	☐	☐	☐	**8**	☐	☐	☐
3	☐	☐	☐	**9**	☐	☐	☐
4	☐	☐	☐	**10**	☐	☐	☐
5	☐	☐	☐	**11**	☐	☐	☐
6	☐	☐	☐	**12**	☐	☐	☐

b   🔊 61 Listen again and repeat the words.

c   🔊 62 Listen and practise saying these sentences.

1 We have to move the sofa.

2 I often have a shower in the evening.

3 I left my scarf in the living room.

4 The film finished at five to eleven.

5 Sofia visits her friends every Friday.

Practise saying these words

🔊 63 bracelet   clothes   early   jacket   jeans   necklace   shorts   skirt   through   tights   trousers   uniform

(5) Listen

a   🔊 64 Listen to three interviews about clothes. What is each person's job?

teacher	business person	doctor	footballer
waitress	actress		

1 Gemma   **2** Luca   **3** Suzanne

....

b   🔊 64 Listen again. What do the people wear for their job? Write G (Gemma), L (Luca) or S (Suzanne) in the boxes. There are three extra pictures.

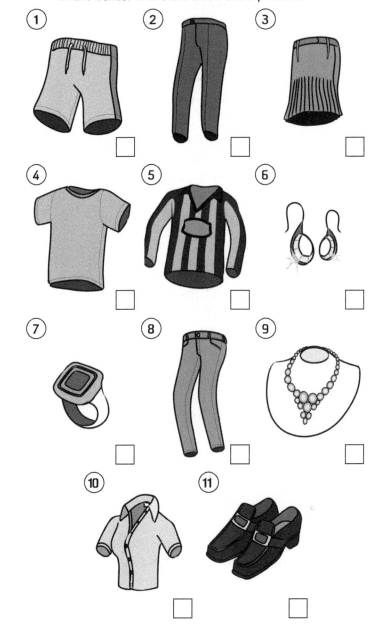

6 Grammar Grammar reference: page 96

can and *could* for requests and permission

a Match the sentences (1–7) with (A–G).

1 ☐ You can wear my jumper if you like.
2 ☐ I can't meet you tonight.
3 ☐ Could I borrow your ruler?
4 ☐ Can we camp here?
5 ☐ We can't go to that disco.
6 ☐ Students can't eat in the classrooms.
7 ☐ Can I phone you later?

A You have to be eighteen.
B It's a school rule.
C It's a nice place for a campsite.
D Dad says I have to do my homework.
E I left mine at home.
F I want to hear about the concert.
G I'm not wearing it tonight.

b There are mistakes in these sentences. Cross out the wrong word(s) and write the correct word(s).

1 You're can put your bike in our garden.   ....
2 We can't to wearing earrings at school.   ....
3 Tony can borrows my football boots.   ....
4 Do we can have a pizza tonight?   ....
5 I don't can go out with you tonight.   ....
6 I could use your phone?   ....

c 🔊 65 Write the questions for these answers. Use the verbs in the box. Then listen and check.

borrow   help   have   speak to

Yes, I'd like to buy a necklace.

No, we're having lunch soon.

1 ....   2 ....

Yes, sure.

No, sorry – Franca isn't here at the moment.

3 ....   4 ....

(7) Read

a Read Myra's internet blog. How many people like school uniforms? ....

By: **myra7**
Posted: 17:16pm   Fri 11 August
We have to wear a boring school uniform and I hate it. It's uncomfortable and it looks awful. Also we can't wear accessories – only a watch. What do other people think about school uniform?

By: **SuperMac**
Posted: 17:45pm   Fri 11 August
I agree, Myra. At my school we have to wear grey trousers and a green jacket and I hate green! 😕 I also hate looking like every other student in the school. The teachers don't have to wear a uniform, so why can't we wear what we want?

By: **alison032**
Posted: 19:02pm   Fri 11 August
Hey come on! Uniforms aren't so bad and you don't have to wear them when you go out. My mum hasn't got a lot of money to spend on clothes. A uniform isn't cheap, but it's more expensive to buy different skirts and trousers all the time.

By: **froggie**
Posted: 20:55pm   Fri 11 August
In the USA some kids have to wear a uniform, but most of us wear normal clothes, like jeans and T-shirts. Who wants to wear the same clothes every day?

By: **jason**
Posted: 1:41pm   Sat 12 August
Ha ha ha! I don't have to wear a uniform.

By: **aishani**
Posted: 16:50pm   Sat 12 August
In India most students wear a school uniform and I think it's OK. It makes me feel like I'm part of the school and there isn't any competition between students about clothes. Our uniform is blue and white and girls can wear a dress or trousers. Everyone looks nice.

b Are the sentences *right* (✓) or *wrong* (✗) or *doesn't say* (–)?

1 Myra can wear a bracelet or a necklace at school. ☐

2 SuperMac doesn't like the colour of his uniform. ☐

3 There are lots of rules at SuperMac's school. ☐

4 Alison says that a uniform doesn't cost much money. ☐

5 Alison isn't interested in clothes. ☐

6 Froggie has to wear jeans every day. ☐

7 Aishani doesn't have to wear a blue and white dress. ☐

c Do you agree with any of the opinions in the blog? Prepare to talk about this in your next class. Make notes to help you.

....

....

....

....

....

Portfolio 10

Add a post to Myra's blog. Write about the clothes and accessories you usually wear at school. If you wear a uniform, say why you like / don't like it. If you don't wear a uniform, say why you think it is/isn't a good idea.

Here are some expressions you can use:

I/We usually/always wear …
We (don't) have to wear …
We can/can't wear …
I (don't) like / love / hate (+ -ing) …

Quiz 10

a What do you remember about Unit 10? Answer all the questions you can and then check in the Student's Book.

1 What colour socks and what colour coat does the boy in picture A wear at school?
....

2 Name three things you can buy in pairs at a shoe shop.
....
....

3 Circle the word that's different.
skirts   shorts   trousers   tights

4 Can you find three types of clothes in picture B?
....
....

5 Write the correct sentence.
He's wearing a black jean, a jumper and a sunglass.
....
....

6 Which sentence is true? Tick (✓) the sentence.
a In the USA you can't drive on the right. ☐
b In the USA you have to drive on the right. ☐
c In the USA you don't have to drive on the right. ☐

7 Put the words in the correct order to make a question.
your / clean / often / to / room / have /
How / you / do ?
....
....

8 Look at the things in picture C and complete the puzzle. What is the ▼ word?

9 You need some money (you can pay it back later). What do you ask your friend?
....

10 Tick (✓) the answer to the question.
A: How much is it?
B: Here you are. ☐
£16.50. ☐
I'll take it. ☐

b 🔊 66 Listen and check.

c Now look at your Student's Book and write two more quiz questions for Unit 10.

Question: ....
....
Answer: ....

Question: ....
....
Answer: ....

1 Vocabulary

Entertainment

a Put the letters in the correct order and write the words in the puzzle. Then use the nine ⃝ letters to make one more type of entertainment.

1 TAHCM

2 CROTCEN

3 MLIF

4 NIXBIOHETI

5 UIMACSL

6 LAYP

7 VILFATSE

R   G

b Write the type of entertainment for each group of words.

1 actor, actress, theatre ....

2 actors, cameras, cinema ....

3 television, channel, sofa ....

4 paintings, drawings, photos ....

5 pop, classical music, jazz ....

6 sport, stadium, competition ....

7 songs, dancing, acting ....

8 holiday, food, fun ....

c Think of an example of each type of entertainment in Exercise 1b. If you can, choose things you have seen yourself.

1 ....

2 ....

3 ....

4 ....

5 ....

6 ....

7 ....

8 ....

2 Grammar

Grammar reference: page 98

Present perfect: statements

a Complete the sentences with the correct form of *have*.

1 You ..’ve........ used this type of camera. Is it easy to use?

2 Their concerts are popular and they .... recorded three albums.

3 I'm not sure what to do. I .... cooked fish before.

4 He's a very famous actor. He .... been in lots of films.

5 Lisa .... eaten carrot soup before. I hope she likes it.

6 We've seen his parents a few times, but we .... spoken to them.

b Write the past participles.

1 She's .... her address five times. (change)

2 My parents have .... in a lot of different jobs. (work)

3 I've never .... cricket. (play)

4 Alex hasn't .... my cousins. (meet)

5 We've .... this CD before. (hear)

6 Julie has .... an art competition. (win)

7 You haven't .... our new dog. He's lovely! (see)

c Complete the sentences with the positive or negative forms of the verbs in the present perfect.

| act | ~~travel~~ | win | eat | take | read |

1 I 've travelled in Africa.

2 She .... in a play before.

3 We .... lots of books.

4 They .... many competitions.

Help yourself!

Irregular past participles

There aren't any rules for irregular past forms, but there are patterns for some verbs.

Write the forms of each verb in the correct table.

| eat | meet | have | see | speak | win |

1 past participle = the same as past simple

Verb	Past simple	Past participle
make	made	made
....	....	....
....	....	....
....	....	....

2 past participle = verb + -n/-en

Verb	Past simple	Past participle
take	took	taken
....	....	....
....	....	....

3 past participle = past simple + -n/-en

Verb	Past simple	Past participle
break	broke	broken
....	....	....

For irregular verbs, learn the verb, past simple and past participle together and revise them often!

5 You .... a lot of photos!

6 He .... Chinese food before.

(3) Vocabulary

Films

a Add vowels (*a, e, i, o, u*) to make words for types of films.

wstrn	mscl	hrrr flm
scnc fctn flm	cmdy	rmnc
drm	nmtd flm	ctn flm

1 ....
2 ....
3 ....
4 ....
5 ....
6 ....
7 ....
8 ....
9 ....

b Complete the sentences with your opinions.

1 The best film I've seen is .... (*name of film*).
It's a .... (*type of film*).

2 The worst film I've seen is .... (*name of film*).
It's a .... (*type of film*).

3 The latest film I've seen is .... (*name of film*).
I saw it .... (*when?*). It's a .... (*type of film*)
and I thought it was .... (*adjective*).

(4) Pronunciation

/ɪ/ and /iː/

a Follow the words with an /iː/ sound to find a way through the puzzle.

→ seen	jeans	quick	<u>ri</u>ver	be<u>gin</u>
give	<u>tea</u>cher	<u>ti</u>cket	<u>li</u>sten	<u>hi</u>story
<u>e</u>vening	maga<u>zine</u>	sand<u>wich</u>	<u>mi</u>rror	chips
cheese	<u>vi</u>sit	CD	Portu<u>guese</u>	key
field	speak	<u>peo</u>ple	<u>bu</u>siness	re<u>peat</u>
<u>bi</u>scuit	fridge	<u>six</u>teen	<u>si</u>lver	<u>free</u>zing →

b 🔊 **67** Listen and check your answers.

c 🔊 **68** Listen and practise saying these word pairs.

	/ɪ/	/iː/
1	bin	been
2	live	leave
3	this	these
4	fit	feet
5	chip	cheap
6	Tim	team

Practise saying these words

🔊 **69** action animated broken competition dream exhibition heard horror match prefer rainforest website

5 Read

a Read the article about an artist. Choose the correct answer: A, B or C.

You can't buy a drawing by Julian Beever and you can't see his work in a gallery or museum. Julian makes his amazing pictures on the pavements of city streets. People have called him 'the Pavement Picasso' and perhaps you've seen his pictures on the internet.

Julian has become famous for his fantastic chalk drawings that look very real when you see them from the right position. He has made hundreds of pieces of 'pavement art' in different countries – in many parts of Europe and also in the USA, Australia, Japan, Argentina and Brazil.

His drawings can take three or four days to finish. But because he draws with chalk, the drawings only stay for a short time. When people walk on them or when it rains, they quickly disappear. For Julian, this isn't a problem. The drawings survive in the photos he has taken, and this is the most important thing for him.

Julian's fame hasn't come from experts in the art world, but from the internet. 'The reason my work has become well known is because people like it and they've sent it to each other on the internet,' he says. 'So I know that what I do is popular.'

Julian Beever is from Leicestershire in England, but he now lives in Belgium.

1 Julian Beever makes drawings
  A outside.
  B on his computer.
  C for exhibitions in a gallery.

2 He has worked
  A in a few cities.
  B in lots of countries.
  C with hundreds of people.

3 His pictures
  A are easy to draw.
  B look good when it rains.
  C don't stay on the pavement.

4 Lots of people know Julian's art because
  A he has sent photos to them.
  B they know a lot about art.
  C they have seen it on the internet.

5 Julian Beever
  A isn't very interested in photos.
  B hasn't tried to be a star in the art world.
  C hasn't lived in Britain.

b Find another picture by Julian Beever on the internet. Prepare to talk about this in your next class. Make notes to help you.

....

....

6 Grammar Grammar reference: page 98

Present perfect: questions

a Make these sentences into questions.

1 I've listened to this programme.
  (you?) Have you listened to this programme?

2 She's worked as a waitress.
  (she?) ....

3 They've had music lessons.
  (they?) ....

4 He's written a play.
  (he?) ....

5 We've been to Turkey.
  (you?) ....

6 Jane's eaten fish soup before.
  (Jane?) ....

b 🔊 **70** Write the questions and complete the answers. Then listen and check.

1 A: you / act / in a play?

....

B: No, ...

2 A: Danny / see / this film?

....

B: Yes, ...

3 A: they / visit / the hospital?

....

B: Yes, ...

4 A: Helen / meet / your parents?

....

B: No, ...

5 A: you and your family / stay / in this hotel?

....

B: No, ...

7 Listen

a 🔊 **70** Listen to three questions from a quiz programme. Who is each question about? Write the person's name and job.

| Julia Roberts | Steven Spielberg | Zac Efron | | director | model | actor |
| Princess Fiona | Cameron Diaz | Indiana Jones | | actress | pop star | songwriter |

Question 1

Name: ....

Present job: ....

Question 2

Name: ....

Present job: ....

Question 3

Name: ....

Present job: ....

b 🔊 **71** Listen again. In each quiz question (1–3), which type(s) of film has the person made? Write 1, 2 or 3 in the boxes.

animated film ☐   TV drama ☐   comedy ☐   horror film ☐   musical ☐

Portfolio 11

Find out about a film director. Write a paragraph and include this information:

• How many films has he/she made?
• What types of films has he/she made?
• What prizes has he/she won?
• What film stars has he/she worked with?
• What is his/her best film, in your opinion?

Check it out!

Use the present perfect when you're talking about <u>any</u> time in the director's life up to now.

If you want to talk about a <u>particular</u> event in the past, use the past simple.

He's made three films with Cate Blanchett. She starred in the first film in 2001.

Quiz (11)

a What do you remember about Unit 11? Answer all the questions you can and then check in the Student's Book.

(A)

(B)

(C)

1 What is the type of entertainment in picture A?

....

2 Can you find two types of entertainment in this puzzle?

| l a v i t s e f h c t a m |

....

3 What are the past participles of these verbs?

play ....
do ....
write ....

4 (Circle) the word that is different.

done   met   ate   spoken

5 There are two mistakes in this sentence. Write the correct sentence.

Kate haven't took any photos with this camera.

....
....

6 (Circle) the two words with the /ɪ/ sound.

violin   magazine   Chinese   history

7 What three types of film can you see in picture B?

....
....

8 Look at the actress in picture C. What was the name of her first film?

....

9 Tick (✓) the correct box for each opinion.

	positive	negative
It was terrible!	☐	☐
It was wonderful!	☐	☐
It was rubbish!	☐	☐

10 (Circle) the correct words.

What is the film *on / for / about*?
What do you think *to / of / on* it?

b 🔊 72 Listen and check.

c Now look at your Student's Book and write two more quiz questions for Unit 11.

Question: ....
....
Answer: ....

Question: ....
....
Answer: ....

12 Party time

1 Vocabulary

Adjectives for feelings

a Write the correct adjectives for feelings under the pictures.

b Complete the sentences with the words in Exercise 1a.

1 It's my little sister's birthday tomorrow. She's very ....

2 I don't like Science. I'm not really .... in it.

3 Some people are .... when they see a spider.

4 I've worked hard all year, so I'm not .... about the exam.

5 I was .... to see Christopher. I thought he was in the USA.

6 There's nothing to do! I'm ....

w _ _ _ _ _ _

f _ _ _ _ _ _ _ _

s _ _ _ _ _ _ _ _

e _ _ _ _ _ _

i _ _ _ _ _ _ _ _ _

b _ _ _ _

Help yourself!

Adjectives from past participles

Adjectives like *worried* and *surprised* are in the form of past participles. Here are some more examples:

an **animated** film
a well-**known** artist

Complete the sentences with adjectives. They are all the past participle form of these verbs.

marry   break   close   wash   grill

1 The dog can't get in. The door is ....

2 Al and Lidia are .... with two children.

3 We had .... steak for dinner.

4 Oh no – look at this! My watch is .... !

5 Don't eat those grapes. They aren't ....

---

2 Grammar Grammar reference: page 100

going to for future plans and intentions

a Write a sentence for each picture.

'm	going to	play	a cake
's		clean	the violin
're		make	my horse
		ride	the bathroom

1 She ....

2 I ....

3 We ....

4 He ....

b 🔊 **73** Read the text and choose the correct answer: A, B or C. Then listen and check.

We've planned everything for the party on Saturday. We ¹...... going to have a lot of food, but ²...... going to buy some pizzas and Isobel ³...... give me her recipe for chocolate cake. Clare ⁴...... going to cook anything, but she and David are going ⁵...... some salads, and Paul ⁶...... going to bring the drinks. We're going ⁷...... all the food on the kitchen table and the music ⁸...... to be in the living room.

	A		B		C	
1	A	don't	B	haven't	C	aren't
2	A	I'm	B	I'm not	C	I've
3	A	is going	B	is going to	C	goes to
4	A	are	B	aren't	C	isn't
5	A	make	B	to make	C	made
6	A	are	B	is	C	isn't
7	A	to throw	B	to sell	C	to put
8	A	is going	B	it's going	C	there's going

c What are these people going to do this afternoon? Use the words to write sentences.

Rachel

1 (go to the stadium)

   She's going to go to the stadium.

2 (watch a football match)

3 (meet a friend)

4 (wear a dress)

Lee and Jason

5 (go surfing)

   They

6 (travel by train)

7 (ride their bikes)

8 (take some food)

d Write the questions with the correct form of *going to* and then write true answers.

1 What / you / do this evening?

4 Who / you / see next weekend?

2 What time / you / get up tomorrow morning?

5 What subjects / you / study next year?

3 What / you / wear tomorrow?

3 Pronunciation

Short forms

a 🔊 74 Listen and repeat.

1 I'll   you'll   he'll   she'll   we'll   they'll
2 I'm   you're   he's   she's   we're   they're

b 🔊 75 Listen and write 1–6 in the boxes.

A ☐ I'll   **B** ☐ I'm   **C** ☐ you'll   **D** ☐ you're

E ☐ they'll   **F** ☐ they're

c 🔊 76 Listen and tick (✓) the sentence you hear: A or B. Then listen again and practise saying the sentences.

1 **A** ☐ You'll bring some decorations.

  B ☐ You're going to bring some decorations.

2 **A** ☐ I'll go and make the coffee.

  B ☐ I'm going to make the coffee.

3 **A** ☐ We'll go and get some bread.

  B ☐ We're going to get some bread.

4 **A** ☐ I'll go and get ready for the party.

  B ☐ I'm going to get ready for the party.

Practise saying these words

🔊 77 burn   busy   frightened   interested
neighbour   noisy   procession   ready   sculpture
surprised   tidy   worried

---

4 Grammar   Grammar reference: page 100

will for offers and spontaneous decisions

a Match the sentences (1–6) with the decisions (A–F).

1 ☐ I'm going to bed now.

2 ☐ They're nice boots, but they're very expensive.

3 ☐ I like this jumper.

4 ☐ The bathroom is very messy.

5 ☐ I want something to eat.

6 ☐ It's sunny outside now.

A I'll clean it before I go to bed.

B I won't take my umbrella.

C I think I'll make a sandwich.

D I won't buy them.

E I'll finish my homework tomorrow.

F I think I'll try it on.

b Look at the pictures and make offers with *I'll*. Use a word from each box.

make   pay for   ~~look~~   wash
help   close

you   floor   window   tickets
coffee   ~~internet~~

We need a train timetable.

1 I'll look on the internet.

It's freezing in here!

2 ....

The kitchen looks awful!

3 ....

I can't move this sofa.

4 ....

Oh no! I haven't got any money!

5 ....

It's very early!

6 ....

⑤ Vocabulary

Celebrations

a Use letters from the three boxes to make eight celebration words.

can dec pro	tu wor es dl	ke nts ion
fire c cos	se ora a	es mes tions
pre gu	cess	ts ks

1 ..candles..............................   5 ....

2 ....   6 ....

3 ....   7 ....

4 ....   8 ....

b Complete the sentences with words in Exercise 5a.

1 People light ..candles.. on the Day of the Dead in Mexico.

2 At the Venice Carnival people wear amazing ....

3 In our village festival there's a .... through the streets.

4 Sydney has wonderful .... to celebrate the New Year.

5 At Chinese New Year you see lots of .... in the streets.

6 At Christmas people give .... to their friends and family.

7 .... often bring flowers when they come to dinner.

8 In many countries people have a special .... when they get married.

⑥ Listen

◁)) **78** Listen to the conversations. Choose the correct answer: A, B or C.

1 How is Ben feeling?

A ☐ B ☐ C ☐

4 What present are they going to get for Alan?

A ☐ B ☐ C ☐

2 What is Kelly going to buy?

A ☐ B ☐ C ☐

5 What does Jill decide to do?

A ☐ B ☐ C ☐

3 What does Jack offer to do?

A ☐ B ☐ C ☐

(7) Read

a Match sentences 1–5 with the correct notices.

A

Barrington Summer Festival

Saturday 28th June

11:00 Boat races
3:30   Procession starting in King Street
8:30   Dinner, Church Square – £14
       Dancing – Black River Band

Fireworks at midnight

B

July Market

**Town Hall car park,
6th July 8:30–12:30**

Fresh local meat, fruit, vegetables
Clothes and jewellery
And lots more!!

C

CONCERT

Abbotsbridge School presents

an exciting programme of
rock, jazz and classical music
at the Princess Theatre

11th July
Admission free

D

FILM CLUB PARTY

11th July, Lansdowne Theatre

come dressed as your favourite film character!
PRIZES FOR THE BEST COSTUMES

Tickets £10

For bookings ring
Jules on 01489 31872

E

Abbots Valley
Basketball Championship Final

Lennox Stadium   **5th July 3:00pm**
Tickets available at the stadium from 27th June

F

Barrington Sports Centre

NEW!

We are starting an aerobics class
on Tuesday evenings.
First class FREE on 1st July
Keep fit and have fun!

G

You are invited to the
Hillway School Art Show

in the school hall

on **Sunday 29 June**

Adults £2   Children free

1 ☐ Everybody is going to wear unusual clothes.

2 ☐ There is going to be an exhibition of painting and sculpture.

3 ☐ This is the earliest event in the year.

4 ☐ You don't have to pay to see the performance.

5 ☐ They've never had this type of activity before.

b Which of these events are similar to events in your town?

....

Portfolio 12

Choose two events from Exercise 7
and write about them in an email to
a friend. Include this information:

- Where are you going to go and when?
- Are you going to meet anyone?
- What are you going to do/see/buy?
- What are you going to wear?

Quiz 12

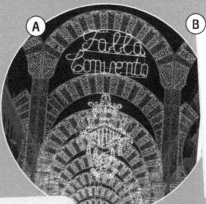

a What do you remember about Unit 12? Answer all the questions you can and then check in the Student's Book.

1 Which city has the festival in picture A?

....

2 (Circle) the correct adjective.

Joanna didn't study for the exam. I wasn't *worried / surprised / excited* when she didn't pass.

3 What is the opposite of *bored*?

....

4 There are two mistakes in this sentence. Write the correct sentence.

I aren't going play hockey this weekend.

....

....

5 Put the words in the correct order to make a question.

are / give / to / his / What / birthday / you / Mike / for / going ?

....

....

6 Choose the correct sentence: A, B or C.

I'm feeling tired.

A I went to bed early.

B I won't go to bed now.

C I think I'll go to bed.

7 Make an offer in answer to this sentence.

A: I'd like to learn to play the guitar.

B: [teach] ....

8 Look at picture B and find three things beginning with *c*.

....

....

9 These are things you give to other people. What are they?

p...

10 Tick (✓) the correct sentence.

How about going to the cinema? ☐

Let's to go to the cinema. ☐

Why we don't go to the cinema? ☐

b 🔊 79 Listen and check.

c Now look at your Student's Book and write two more quiz questions for Unit 12.

Question: ....

....

Answer: ....

Question: ....

....

Answer: ....

Grammar reference

1 Plural nouns

● The ending of a plural noun is usually -s.

day → days   friend → friends   computer → computers

● Nouns ending in -s, -sh, -ch or -x: the ending is -es.

bus → buses   class → classes   dish → dishes
sandwich → sandwiches   match → matches   box → boxes

● Nouns ending in a consonant + -y: the ending is -ies.

family → families   city → cities

● Nouns ending in -f or -fe: the ending is usually -ves.

shelf → shelves   scarf → scarves   wife → wives

● Some nouns are irregular in the plural.

woman → **women**
man → **men**
child → **children**
person → **people**

> ✱ Some nouns haven't got a plural form. See Countable and uncountable nouns, page 92.
>
> Some nouns are always plural: *jeans, trousers, shorts, sunglasses.*

2 The verb *be*

Positive			Negative		
I	**'m (am)**	Italian.	I	**'m not (am not)**	Italian.
He/She/It	**'s (is)**		He/She/It	**isn't (is not)**	
You/We/They	**'re (are)**		You/We/They	**aren't (are not)**	
Yes/No questions			**Short answers**		
Am	I	Italian?	Yes, I **am**.	No, I **'m not**.	
Is	he/she/it		Yes, he/she/it **is**.	No, he/she/it **isn't**.	
Are	you/we/they		Yes, you/we/they **are**.	No, you/we/they **aren't**.	
Information questions					
How **are** you? Where**'s** Emma? What **are** your favourite songs? Who**'s** your best friend?					

● We can also use these negative forms:

you're not (= you aren't)   he's not (= he isn't)
we're not (= we aren't)   she's not (= she isn't)
they're not (= they aren't)   it's not (= it isn't)

● For questions with the verb *be*, only the word order changes. We don't use *do* or *does* with this verb.

It's hot outside.   **Is** *it hot outside?*
*The eggs **are** in the fridge.*   **Are** *the eggs in the fridge?*   *Where **are** the eggs?*
He's angry.   *Why **is** he angry?*

Grammar practice

1 Plural nouns

Write the plural nouns.

1 _bikes_

2 ....

3 ....

4 ....

5 ....

6 ....

7 ....

8 ....

9 ....

2 The verb *be*

a There is a mistake in each line of these conversations. ~~Cross out~~ the wrong word(s) and write the correct word(s).

1 A: Hi! How ~~you are~~?   _are you_ ....

   B: I fine, thanks.   ....

2 A: Pietro is a student?   ....

   B: Yes, he does.   ....

3 A: Where my phone is?   ....

   B: Is on the table.   ....

4 A: Your name is it Angela?   ....

   B: Yes, I am.   ....

5 A: Where's Mum and Dad?   ....

   B: They in the garden.   ....

b Complete the phone conversation. Use the correct form of the verb *be*.

Petra: Hi, Alex. How [1]................ things?

Alex: Not bad. Where [2]................ you?

Petra: I [3]................ at the White Lion Café.

Alex: [4]................ Elizabeth with you?

Petra: No, she [5]................ here. I [6]................ with Javier and Cristina.

Alex: Yeah? Who [7]................ they?

Petra: They [8]................ my cousins from Portugal. Can you come to the café?

Alex: What time [9]................ it now?

Petra: It [10]................ half past ten.

Alex: OK. See you soon.

Grammar reference

(3) ## There is / There are

Positive and negative			
There	**'s (is)**	a cinema	
	are	two cinemas some cinemas lots of cinemas	in this town.
	isn't (is not)	a cinema	
	aren't (are not)	any cinemas	

Yes/No questions			Short answers	
Is	**there**	a cinema?	Yes, **there is.**	No, **there isn't.**
Are		any cinemas?	Yes, **there are.**	No, **there aren't.**

There's a café next to the post office.   *There aren't* any eggs in the fridge.
Is there a station near your school?   How many students **are there** in your class?

---

(4) ## this / that / these / those

This is **That**'s	my cat. my village.	*(It's near me.)* *(It's at a distance from me.)*
These are **Those** are	my friends. my parents.	*(They're near me.)* *(They're at a distance from me.)*

- *This*, *that*, *these* and *those* can stand alone or they can go before a noun.

  This is a boring film.   **This** <u>film</u> is boring.
  Those are nice shoes.   I really like **those** <u>shoes</u>.

This is my cat.   That's my village.

---

(5) ## have got

Positive			Negative		
I/You/We/They	**'ve got (have got)**	a computer. brown eyes.	I/You/We/They	**haven't got (have not got)**	a computer. brown eyes.
He/She/It	**'s got (has got)**		He/She/It	**hasn't got (has not got)**	

Yes/No questions				Short answers	
Have	I/you/we/they	**got**	a computer? brown eyes?	Yes, I/you/we/they **have.**	No, I/you/we/they **haven't.**
Has	he/she/it			Yes, he/she/it **has.**	No, he/she/it **hasn't.**

- We use *have got* to say that things belong to people.

  He's got a piano.
  I've got two brothers.
  We haven't got a swimming pool.
  Has Sonia got blonde hair?

- We don't use *do* or *does* with *have got*.

  I haven't got a dog. (**not** ~~I don't have got~~)   *Have you got a phone?* (**not** ~~Do you have got~~)

> ✱ It is possible to use the verb *have* instead of *have got*.
>
> *He has a piano.   Does she have blonde hair?*
> This is normal in US English.

Grammar practice

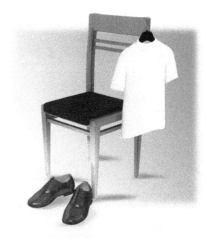

3 *There is / There are*

a Complete the sentences. Use the words in the box with
there + *'s/isn't/are/aren't*.

> hat   T-shirt   shoes   jeans

.... a white .... in the picture, but
.... any ....
.... a .... , but .... two
black ....

b Complete the questions and write the answers.

1 ..Is there.. a chair in the picture?   ....
2 .... a table?   ....
3 .... any people in the picture?   ....
4 How many shoes ....?   ....

4 *this/that/these/those*

Complete the sentences with *this*, *that*, *these* or *those*.

Is .... your teacher?

Look at ....!

.... are my new jeans.

Are .... dogs friendly?

.... strawberries are nice.

.... film was really bad!

5 *have got*

Write sentences with *have got*.

1 We / a new television
   ....

2 Joanna / blue eyes
   ....

3 I / not / a piano
   ....

4 Tony / not / long hair
   ....

5 you / a dictionary?
   ....

6 What / they / in that box?
   ....

7 How many brothers and sisters / Carla?
   ....

Grammar reference

6 Pronouns and possessive adjectives

Subject pronouns	Object pronouns	Possessive adjectives
I	me	my
you	you	your
he	him	his
she	her	her
it	it	its
we	us	our
they	them	their

Subject and object pronouns

Mike loves carrots.   ***He*** *loves* ***them***.
Kate and I saw Nadia.   ***We*** *saw* ***her***.
Are you looking for Ben?   *Are you looking for* ***him***?
Listen to Danny and me!   *Listen to* ***us***!
I gave the CDs to Lisa.   *I gave* ***them*** *to* ***her***.

Mike is eating carrots.
He loves them.

Possessive adjectives

● Possessive adjectives always come before a noun. Their form doesn't change.

  <u>David</u> was at the party with **his** brother and **his** cousin Sara.
  <u>Anna and Jill</u> are in Lisbon. **Their** hotel is nice but **their** rooms are quite small.

● We use *its* for things, animals and places.

  <u>Put the DVD</u> back in **its** box.
  <u>The bird</u> is sitting on **its** eggs.
  <u>Germany</u> is in Europe. **Its** biggest city is Berlin.

> ✱ Don't confuse *its* (= possessive adjective) with *it's* (= *it is* or *it has*).

7 Possessive 's

● We use an apostrophe (') with a noun to show possession.

● Singular and irregular plural nouns: add *'s*.

  <u>Helen</u>**'s** books   <u>Marco</u>**'s** address   my <u>brother</u>**'s** room
  the <u>children</u>**'s** toys   the <u>women</u>**'s** basketball team

● Plural nouns ending in -*s*: add only an apostrophe (').

  the <u>students</u>**'** names (= the names of the students)
  my <u>brothers</u>**'** room (= the room of my brothers)

> ✱ If two people own something, only the second name is in the possessive form.
> *That's* ***Sam and Martha's*** *house.*
> (**not** ~~Sam's~~ and Martha's)

my brother's room

my brothers' room

Grammar practice

6 Pronouns and possessive adjectives

a (Circle) the correct pronoun.

1 Teresa's lucky. *She / Her* goes skiing every winter.

2 Our grandparents often have lunch with *we / us*.

3 I don't want this hamburger – *it / he* isn't very nice.

4 You can have these earrings. I never wear *it / them*.

5 *We / Us* don't go to school on Saturdays.

6 That's Peter. I sit next to *he / him* at school.

b Complete the sentences with pronouns.

1 That's our football. Give it to .us. !

2 This is my new camera. Dad gave it to .... for my birthday.

3 Those are Annie's sunglasses. Please give them to ....

4 A: Can I borrow your necklace for the party?

   B: Yes, OK. I'll give it to .... tomorrow.

5 This book is for Ricardo. Could you give it to ...., please?

6 We haven't got your keys. You didn't give .... to ....

Give it to us!

c Complete the sentences with possessive adjectives.

1 What do you want for ..your.. birthday?

2 Hello. .... name's Carolina and I'm from Brazil.

3 I can't phone Steve. I haven't got .... number.

4 We live in Prague. .... flat is near the river.

5 Antonia's mother is an actress and .... father is a painter.

6 We can't use this chair. .... leg is broken.

7 Did you finish .... homework last night?

8 My sisters are watching *The Simpsons*. It's .... favourite TV programme.

7 Possessive 's

Rewrite the sentences. Use the possessive 's.

1 Julie has got a black cat.   Julie's cat is black. ....

2 Carl has got a red guitar.   ....

3 The children have got a small bedroom.   ....

4 My cousins have got a Polish surname.   ....

5 My aunt has got a Japanese car.   ....

6 Our teacher has got very short hair.   ....

7 The players have got yellow shirts.   ....

8 My friend has got a really nice jacket. ....

9 Australia has got beautiful beaches.   ....

10 Their parents have got a very old computer.   ....

Grammar reference

(8) Present simple

Positive			Negative			
I/You/We/They	**live**	in Spain.	I/You/We/They	**don't (do not)**	**live**	in Spain.
He/She/It	**lives**		He/She/It	**doesn't (does not)**		
Yes/No questions			**Short answers**			
Do	I/you/we/they	**live**	Yes, I/you/we/they **do**.	No, I/you/we/they **don't**.		
Does	he/she/it	in Spain?	Yes, he/she/it **does**.	No, he/she/it **doesn't**.		
Information questions						
Where **do** you **live**? What time **do** they **have** lunch? How often **does** he **play** tennis?						

- With *he/she/it*, the verb ends in *-s*.

  *he speak**s**   she play**s**   it move**s***

  Verbs ending in *-s*, *-sh*, *-ch*, *-x* and *-o*: the ending is *-es*.

  *he miss**es**   she wash**es**   he watch**es**   she relax**es**   he do**es**   it go**es***

  Verbs ending in a consonant + *-y*: the ending is *-ies*.

  *he worr**ies**   she stud**ies**   it fl**ies***

- The form for the verb *have* is *has* (**not** ~~haves~~).

  *She **has** a shower.   Karl **has** breakfast.*

- We use *do/does* for questions and *don't/doesn't* for negatives.

- We use the present simple for permanent situations, regular or repeated actions, and facts.

  *My father **works** in a hospital.*
  *We **walk** to school every morning.*
  *She **doesn't speak** Russian.*
  ***Do** you **like** olives?*

- We often use these time expressions with the present simple:

  every day, every morning, every week
  in the morning, in the evening, at night
  on Sundays, on Tuesdays
  at the weekend

My father works in a hospital.

(9) Adverbs of frequency

0%   100%

never   hardly ever   sometimes   often   usually   always

- Adverbs of frequency usually go before the verb.

  *We **sometimes** <u>play</u> tennis at the weekend.*
  *My sister **never** <u>gets up</u> early.*
  *Do you **often** <u>go</u> to the cinema?*

  > ✱ For the position of other adverbs, see Adverbs of manner on page 88.

- However, they go after the verb *be*.

  *Tony <u>is</u> **always** late for school.*
  *It<u>'s</u> **hardly ever** cold in the summer.*
  *I<u>'m</u> **usually** in bed before midnight.*

- Remember to use a positive verb with *never* and *hardly ever*.

  We never go camping. (**not** ~~don't never go~~)
  I hardly ever eat meat. (**not** ~~don't hardly ever eat~~)

Grammar practice

8 Present simple

Complete the conversations with the verbs in the present simple.

leave	work	be	get up	do	like	not see

A: Where [1]_____ your mother _____?

B: In the city. She [2]_____ home before Dad and I [3]_____,
   so we [4]_____ her in the morning on weekdays.

A: What [5]_____ she _____?

B: She [6]_____ a bus driver.

A: _____ she [7]_____ her job?

B: Yes, she loves driving and she's really good at it.

come	like	walk	teach	not speak	not say	not know	not be

A: I [8]_____ that man. Who is he?

B: That's our neighbour, Mr Lambert. He [9]_____ French at Matt's school.

A: [10]_____ you _____ him?

B: Yes, he's very nice, but his wife [11]_____ very friendly. She [12]_____
   past our house every day but she [13]_____ hello.

A: Maybe she [14]_____ English.

B: Oh yes, she does. I know her family. She [15]_____ from London.

9 Adverbs of frequency

a Rewrite the sentences with the adverbs of frequency.

1 Schools teach Japanese in my country. (hardly ever)

   Schools hardly ever teach Japanese in my country.

2 I go to the sports centre on Sundays. (sometimes)

   ....

3 The food is very good at that restaurant. (never)

   ....

4 Dad is very tired after work. (often)

   ....

5 Do you do your homework in the evening? (usually)

   ....

6 There are thousands of people at the festival. (always)

   ....

b Rewrite the sentences. Change the <u>underlined</u> words to adverbs of frequency.

1 Dad cooks <u>two or three times a week</u>.   Dad sometimes cooks.

2 The cat is outside <u>nearly all the time</u>.   ....

3 We play football <u>four or five times a week</u>. ....

4 A: How's Ellie?
  B: I don't know. I see her <u>only twice a year</u>. ....

5 Music lessons are interesting <u>all the time</u>. ....

6 I <u>don't</u> read history books <u>at any time</u>. ....

Grammar reference

(10) Present continuous

Positive			Negative		
I	**'m (am)**		I	**'m not (am not)**	
He/She/It	**'s (is)**	**walking**.	He/She/It	**isn't (is not)**	**walking**.
You/We/They	**'re (are)**		You/We/They	**aren't (are not)**	
Yes/No questions			**Short answers**		
Am	I		Yes, I **am**.	No, I**'m not**.	
Is	he/she/it	**walking**?	Yes, he/she/it **is**.	No, he/she/it **isn't**.	
Are	you/we/they		Yes, you/we/they **are**.	No, you/we/they **aren't**.	
Information questions					
Where **are** you **going**? What**'s** she **doing**? Why **are** those people **shouting**?					

- For the present continuous we use *am/is/are* + verb + *-ing*.

- We can also use these negative forms:

  you're not / we're not / they're not walking
  he's not / she's not / it's not walking

> ✱ For spelling of the *-ing* form, see Verb + *-ing* on page 88.

- We don't normally use the present continuous for these verbs:

  like   love   hate   prefer   want   need   know   understand

  Do you **like** this cheese? (**not** ~~Are you liking~~)
  I **don't know** the answer to that question. (**not** ~~I'm not knowing~~)

Present meaning

- We use the present continuous for actions happening now and for temporary actions.

  *Hey, look! It**'s snowing**!*
  *Hurry up! The taxi**'s waiting**.*
  *I**'m reading** a book about Africa.*
  *How many subjects **are** you **studying** this year?*

It's snowing!

- We often use these time expressions with the present meaning of the present continuous:

  now, at the moment
  this morning, this week, this year

> ✱ We don't use adverbs of frequency with the present continuous.

Future meaning

- We also use the present continuous to talk about future arrangements, often in the near future.

  *I**'m going** to the beach this afternoon.*
  *Robbie**'s meeting** us outside the cinema at 7:30.*
  *What **are** you **doing** tomorrow night?*

I'm going to the beach.

- We often use these time expressions with the future meaning of the present continuous:

  soon
  tomorrow, tomorrow morning, tomorrow night
  on Friday
  in February
  next week, next weekend, next month

Grammar practice

10 Present continuous

a) Complete the phone conversations with the verbs in the present continuous.

Present meaning

work	sit	do	help	try	teach	not use

A: What ¹_____ you _____?

B: My homework!

A: Me too. ²_____ you _____ on the Geography project?

B: Yes, I ³_____ to find some information on the internet. What about you?

A: Oh, I've got some books from my sister, so I ⁴_____ the computer right now.

B: ⁵_____ your sister _____ you?

A: Not at the moment. She and Dad ⁶_____ in the car outside our house. He ⁷_____ her to drive.

Future meaning

do	go	have	meet	help	play	watch	not go out

A: Silvia phoned a few minutes ago. She ⁸_____ me at the bridge after lunch and we ⁹_____ to the swimming pool. Do you want to come?

B: No, I ¹⁰_____ this afternoon. I ¹¹_____ the football. Manchester and Chelsea ¹²_____ .

A: Oh, OK. What about Martin? What ¹³_____ he _____ this afternoon?

B: I think he ¹⁴_____ his parents at home. They ¹⁵_____ a big family party tonight.

b) Complete the sentences. Use the present continuous or the present simple.

1 A: You _____ (wear) your new shirt! It looks great.

   B: Yes, I _____ (love) it. It's really comfortable.

2 A: _____ Elise _____ (want) to go shopping with us?

   B: No, she _____ (study) at the moment.

3 A: _____ you _____ (enjoy) your pasta?

   B: Yes, it's good. I _____ often _____ (not eat) Italian food, but this is delicious.

4 A: _____ Carlo usually _____ (work) during the summer holidays?

   B: Yes, but he _____ (not look) for a job this year.

5 A: I _____ (have) problems with this exercise. _____ you _____ (know) the answer?

   B: No, I _____ (not understand) the question.

Grammar reference

11 Verb + -ing

- After *like, love, hate* and *enjoy* we often use a verb + -ing.

  We enjoy **playing** basketball.
  She hates **tidying** her room.
  Do you like **skiing**?

  > ✳ We can also use a noun or pronoun after these verbs.
  > *I don't like this music.*
  > *I don't like it.*

  Spelling of the -ing form

- Verbs ending in -e: ~~e~~ + -ing.

  I love riding my bike. (**not** ~~rideing~~)
  They don't like dancing. (**not** ~~danceing~~)

- Short verbs ending in one vowel + a consonant: double consonant + -ing.

  He enjoys swi**mm**ing.
  Do they like ru**nn**ing?

- Verbs ending in -ie: ~~ie~~ + -ying.

  He's lying on his bed. (**not** ~~lieing~~)
  These flowers are dying. (**not** ~~dieing~~)

  > ✳ We can also use the -ing form after *be good at* and *be bad at*.
  > *You're good at painting.*
  > *I'm bad at singing.*

12 Adverbs of manner

Regular		Irregular	
Adjective	**Adverb**	**Adjective**	**Adverb**
sad	sad**ly**	good	**well**
quick	quick**ly**	hard	**hard**
loud	loud**ly**	fast	**fast**
		early	**early**
easy	eas**ily**	late	**late**
happy	happ**ily**		

- An adverb of manner goes with a verb to describe an action.

- Adverbs of manner normally go after the verb (and the object if there is one).

  They<u>'re talking</u> **loudly**.
  He <u>doesn't drive</u> **carefully**.
  We <u>left</u> the house **quietly**.

  > ✳ However, adverbs of frequency normally go <u>before</u> the verb. See Adverbs of frequency on page 84.

- For most adverbs of manner, the form is adjective + -ly.

- Adjectives ending in -y: ~~y~~ + -ily.

- Some adverbs are irregular.

  They sing **well**.
  I'm working **hard**.
  Can you run **fast**?

  > ✳ Not all words ending in -ly are adverbs of manner. These words are adjectives, not adverbs:
  > *lovely   lonely   friendly   unfriendly*

Grammar practice

11 Verb + -ing

Complete the sentences. Use *love*, *enjoy*, *not like* or *hate* with a verb + -ing.

1 She _____ horror films.

2 He _____ football.

3 They _____ .

4 I _____ a hat.

12 Adverbs of manner

a There is a mistake in each sentence. ~~Cross out~~ the wrong word(s) and write the correct word(s).

1 The bus often arrives ~~lately~~.   late

2 This isn't difficult – I can do it easy.   _____

3 James is studying very hardly at the moment.   _____

4 It's very foggy. Please slowly drive.   _____

5 I'm going to bed early tonight.   _____

6 Read the exam questions carefully.   _____

7 Our team played very good on Saturday.   _____

b Make adverbs from these adjectives and complete the sentences.

happy	~~fast~~	hard	bad	good	loud

1 He 's riding fast .

2 They're working _____ .

3 She's talking _____ .

4 She's surfing _____ .

5 They're playing _____ .

6 He's acting _____ .

Grammar reference

13. Past simple: the verb *be*

Positive			Negative		
I/He/She/It	**was**	cold.	I/He/She/It	**wasn't (was not)**	cold.
You/We/They	**were**		You/We/They	**weren't (were not)**	
Yes/No questions			Short answers		
Was	I/he/she/it	cold?	Yes, I/he/she/it **was**.	No, I/he/she/it **wasn't**.	
Were	you/we/they		Yes, you/we/they **were**.	No, you/we/they **weren't**.	
Information questions					
Where **were** they yesterday? Why **was** she late? When **were** you born?					

- For questions with the verb *be*, only the word order changes. We don't use *did* with this verb.

  They **were** *here yesterday.*   *When* **were** <u>*they*</u> *here?*   <u>*The film*</u> **was** *good.*   **Was** <u>*the film*</u> *good?*

14. Past simple

Positive			Negative		
I/You/We/They/He/She/It	**worked.** **left.**		I/You/We/They/He/She/It	**didn't (did not)**	**work.** **leave.**
Yes/No questions			Short answers		
Did	I/you/we/they/he/she/it	**work?** **leave?**	Yes, I/you/we/they/he/she/it **did**. No, I/you/we/they/he/she/it **didn't**.		
Information questions					
What time **did** you **leave**? Where **did** he **go** last night? When **did** they **arrive**?					

- We use the past simple for completed actions in the past.

Regular verbs

- The ending for most verbs in the past simple is *-ed*. The form is the same for all subjects.

  I **finished** *the book yesterday.*   *We* **finished** *our lunch at 1:30.*   *The film* **finished** *late.*

- We use *did* for questions and *didn't* for negatives. The form is the same for all subjects.

  When **did** *your exams* **finish**?   *He* **didn't play** *football last weekend.*

Spelling of the *-ed* form

- Verbs ending in *-e*: add *-d*: *like → liked, decide → decided.*

- Short verbs ending in one vowel + a consonant: double consonant + *-ed*: *stop → sto**pp**ed, plan → pla**nn**ed.*

- Verbs ending in a consonant + *-y*: *~~y~~ + -ied*: *try → tr**ied**, hurry → hurr**ied**.*

Irregular verbs

- Some verbs are irregular.

  have → **had**, *see →* **saw**, *buy →* **bought**.

  However, they follow the normal rules for negatives and questions.

  I **didn't have** *lunch.*   **Did** *you* **see** *me?*   *What* **did** *she* **buy**?

  ✱ For a list of irregular verbs, see page 102.

- We often use these time expressions with the past simple:

  yesterday, last night, last week, last weekend, last year
  two hours ago, three days ago, a few weeks ago, a year ago

  ✱ Note:
  <u>*yesterday*</u> *morning/afternoon/evening*
  <u>*last*</u> *night*

Grammar practice

13 Past simple: the verb *be*

Complete the sentences with the past simple form of *be* (positive or negative).

1 I remember my first day at primary school. I _____ very excited.

2 Where are my keys? They _____ here a minute ago.

3 Sara started playing the violin in 2002. She _____ eight years old.

4 We didn't eat much for breakfast. We _____ hungry.

5 I didn't see you at the match yesterday. Where _____ you?

6 Amy _____ born in the UK. She and her family are from Canada.

7 Tony didn't get to school until 10:30. Why _____ he late?

8 Was it a good party? _____ there many people?

14 Past simple

a Write the negative and question forms of these sentences.

1 He walked home with Alice.

   He didn't walk home with Alice.

   Did he walk home with Alice?

2 You tried to help him.

   _____

   _____

3 The train stopped at Cambridge.

   _____

   _____

4 They recorded the song in 2005.

   _____

   _____

5 Chris stayed in Tokyo last year.

   _____

   _____

b Complete the crossword with the past simple form of the verbs.

Across →	Down ↓
4 come	1 make
7 eat	2 leave
9 think	3 go
10 lose	5 begin
	6 tell
	8 take

c There is a mistake in each past sentence. ~~Cross out~~ the wrong word(s) and write the correct word(s).

1 On Saturday we watch an interesting film on TV. _____

2 Mum takes my little brother to the doctor's yesterday. _____

3 I finished my homework when I get up this morning. _____

4 Kate's parents were at the concert but I not met them. _____

5 What had you for dinner last night? _____

6 My grandfather studied Russian when he was at school. _____

7 We went to the supermarket and buoght some food. _____

8 I didn't send him an email because I didn't knew his address. _____

9 What time the postman came this morning? _____

10 I see Renata yesterday but I didn't talk to her. _____

Grammar reference

15. Countable and uncountable nouns

- Most nouns are countable – they are things we can count. They have a singular and a plural form.

  a computer   computers   two computers   an egg   eggs   six eggs

- Uncountable nouns have only a singular form. We don't use *a* or *an* with these nouns.

  We're listening to music.   I love Chinese food.

- Some common uncountable nouns:

  music   time   money   food   bread   rice   cheese   meat   fruit   water   milk

- Sometimes a noun can be countable or uncountable.

  *There's **some coffee** in the kitchen.* (uncountable)   *I love **fish**.* (= type of food, uncountable)
  *Would you like **a coffee**?* (= a cup of coffee, countable)   *That's **a big fish**!* (= an animal, countable)

16. *a/an*, *some* and *any*

	Countable nouns		Uncountable nouns
	singular	plural	
I've got	a sandwich.	**some** sandwiches.	**some** cheese.
He hasn't got	a sandwich.	**any** sandwiches.	**any** cheese.
Have you got	a sandwich?	**any** sandwiches?	**any** cheese?

- We use *a/an* only with singular countable nouns.

  There's a banana on the table. (**not** ~~a bread, a rice, a water~~)
  I need an onion for the soup. (**not** ~~an oil~~)

- We use *some* and *any* to talk about an indefinite number or quantity. We use them with plural nouns and uncountable nouns.

- We use *some* in positive sentences. We normally use *any* in negative sentences and questions.

  *She bought **some** shoes.*   *She bought **some** ham.*
  *I don't want **any** grapes.*   *I don't want **any** fruit.*
  *Have you got **any** eggs?*   *Have you got **any** milk?*

17. *a lot of*, *much* and *many*

	Plural countable nouns	Uncountable nouns
They've got	**a lot of** DVDs.	**a lot of** money.
I haven't got	**many** DVDs.	**much** money.
Have you got	**many** DVDs?	**much** money?

- We use *a lot of*, *much* and *many* to talk about a large number or quantity.

- In positive sentences we normally use *a lot of*.

  *There were **a lot of** people at the beach.*   *There's **a lot of** oil in this salad.*

  > ✱ We can also use *lots of*.
  > *lots of people   lots of oil*

- We normally use *much* and *many* in negative sentences and questions. *Much* goes with uncountable nouns and *many* goes with plural nouns.

  *I don't eat **many** potatoes.*   *I don't eat **much** meat.*
  *Has he got **many** friends?*   *Does he drink **much** coffee?*
  *How **many** subjects do you study?*   *How **much** time have we got?*

Grammar practice

15 Countable and uncountable nouns

Write the words. Use *a/an* if the noun is countable.

1 ...chocolate........   2 ...an egg...........   3 ....   4 ....   5 ....

6 ....   7 ....   8 ....   9 ....   10 ....

16 *a/an, some* and *any*

a (Circle) the correct word.

1 Have we got *some / any* rice?
2 I'd like *some / any* olives on my pizza.
3 There isn't *some / any* salt in this soup.
4 Let's listen to *some / any* music.

5 Are there *some / any* apples on the table?
6 I don't need *some / any* onions for this recipe.
7 He bought *some / any* new jeans.

b Complete the sentences with *a, an, some* or *any*.

1 We need .... cheese to go with the pasta.
2 I'm reading .... interesting book at the moment.
3 We haven't got .... homework this weekend.
4 Have you seen .... films by Steven Spielberg?

5 Jill got .... tickets for the concert.
6 Have they got .... new car?
7 There aren't .... good singers in that band.

17 *a lot of, much* and *many*

Complete the sentences with *much, many* or *a lot of.*

A: Hi, Mum. I'm with Angelo. Can he have dinner with us tonight?

B: Well, I've got ¹.......................... vegetables here, but there isn't ².......................... meat. Can you go to the supermarket?

A: OK, but I haven't got ³.......................... money.

B: How ⁴.......................... have you got?

A: About £5.

B: That's OK. I don't want ⁵.......................... things. Just some more chicken and some eggs.

A: How ⁶.......................... eggs do you need?

B: Six. And get some strawberries if you can. They had ⁷.......................... cheap strawberries at the supermarket yesterday.

A: OK, Mum. See you soon.

Grammar reference

18 Comparative and superlative adjectives

Adjective	Comparative	Superlative
old	**older**	the **oldest**
nice	**nicer**	the **nicest**
big	**bigger**	the **biggest**
heavy	**heavier**	the **heaviest**
beautiful	**more beautiful**	the **most beautiful**
important	**more important**	the **most important**

Regular forms

● For short adjectives, the ending is *-er* for the comparative and *-est* for the superlative.

*I'm **younger** than my sister Cathy. She's 19.*
*My brother Tom is 11. He's **the youngest** person in my family.*

● For longer adjectives, we use *more* for the comparative and *the most* for the superlative.

*I think the book was **more interesting** than the film.*
*I enjoy all my subjects, but Science is **the most interesting**.*

Spelling of *-er* and *-est* forms

● Adjectives ending in *-e*: add *-r* or *-st*.

strange → stranger, strangest   nice → nicer, nicest

● Adjectives of one syllable ending in one vowel + a consonant: double consonant + *-er, -est*.

big → bigger, biggest   hot → hotter, hottest

● Adjectives ending in *-y*: ~~y~~ + *-ier, -iest*.

sunny → sunnier, sunniest   noisy → noisier, noisiest

Irregular forms

● Some adjectives are irregular in the comparative and superlative.

good → better, the best
bad → worse, the worst
far → further, the furthest

*Sam is a **better** actor than Daniel.   Karen is **the best** player in the team.*

19 Prepositions of place

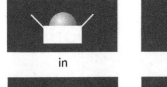

in   on   opposite   in front of

under   behind   next to   between

*I live **in** a flat / **in** Paris / **in** France.*
*The clock is **on** the desk / **on** the wall.*
*There's a cupboard **under** the stairs.*
*You can't see her because she's **behind** the tree.*

*We live **opposite** the station.*
*The teacher is standing **in front of** the class.*
*There's a table **next to** my bed.*
*The café is **between** the bank and the chemist's.*

Grammar practice

18 Comparative and superlative adjectives

a Write sentences with the comparative form of the adjectives.

① Melanie Jill

②

③

④ £45 £75

⑤

⑥

1 (tall) Melanie is taller than Jill. ....

2 (big) ....

3 (heavy) ....

4 (expensive) ....

5 (bad) ....

6 (comfortable) ....

b Complete the sentences with the superlative form of these adjectives.

> boring ~~short~~ hot noisy difficult good

1 Mum is only 152 cm tall. She's the shortest person in our family.

2 Why are you watching that rubbish? It's .... programme on TV!

3 I really love football. It's .... sport in the world.

4 In Europe, ... months are usually July and August.

5 I'm not very good at Maths and Science. They're .... subjects for me.

6 This is .... street in our town. It's never quiet.

19 Prepositions of place

Look at the picture and complete the text with prepositions.

Mr and Mrs Brown live ¹ opposite our house, ² .... the bookshop and the newsagent's. At the moment they're both ³ .... their garden. Mrs Brown is sitting ⁴ .... a chair ⁵ .... the tree and her husband is standing ⁶ .... her. Their dog Bilbo is ⁷ .... Mrs Brown and I can see their cat ⁸ .... the tree.

Grammar reference

20 *can*

Positive			Negative		
I/You/We/They/He/She/It	**can**	**swim**.	I/You/We/They/He/She/It	**can't (cannot)**	**swim**.
Yes/No questions			**Short answers**		
Can	I/you/we/they/he/she/it	**swim**?	Yes, I/you/we/they/he/she/it **can**. No, I/you/we/they/he/she/it **can't**.		
Information questions					
Who **can** you **see**? What languages **can** Olga **speak**? What time **can** they **come**?					

- The form *can* + verb is the same for all subjects.

  I **can** speak English.   Mike **can** play the guitar.

- We don't use *do* or *does* for negatives or questions.

  Penguins **can't** fly.   **Can** you hear me?

Ability

- We use *can* + verb to talk about people's abilities.

  Joe **can** ride a bike.   I **can't** swim very well.

- The past form of *can* is *could*.

  My sister **could** read when she was three years old.   I **couldn't** sleep last night.

Requests and permission

- We can use *can* + verb to ask for something (making a request).

  Can I have a kilo of onions, please?
  Can I have the salt, please?

- We can use *can* + verb to ask for and give permission.

  Can I go to the party, Mum?   **Can** I try on your sunglasses?   **Can** we borrow your camera, please?
  You **can** go out when you finish your homework.   We **can't** use dictionaries during the exam.

- In questions making requests or asking for permission, we can use *can* or *could*. In these questions, *could* doesn't have a past meaning. It means the same as *can* but it is more formal.

  Jane, **can** I have a look at the menu?   Excuse me, **could** I have a menu, please?

21 *I'd like … / Would you like … ?*

I'd like (I would like)	six lemons, please. to buy these earrings.
Would you like	a piece of cake? to sit next to the window?

> ✱ Don't confuse *I'd like* (= *I want*) with *I like*. See Verb + *-ing* on page 88.

- We can use *would like* before a noun or before *to* + verb.

- We use *I'd like* to ask for something and *Would you like … ?* to offer something. This form is more polite than *I want / Do you want … ?*

Grammar practice

20 can

a Make sentences with *can/can't* and the verbs in the box.

> sing   ride   speak   ~~make~~   not drive   not play

1 I / a chocolate cake

  I can make a chocolate cake.

2 you / a horse?

....

3 she / the piano

....

4 he / four languages

....

5 they / this song?

....

6 I / a car

....

b Ask for permission with *Can* and *Could*.

1 You and your friend want to go to the library. Ask your teacher.

  Could we go to the library?

2 You want to use your friend's phone. Ask him/her.

....

3 You are in a bus and you want to open the window. Ask the person next to you.

....

4 You are in a shop and you want to try on some jeans. Ask the shop assistant.

....

5 You are in class and you need to borrow a rubber. Ask the student next to you.

....

6 Your family is going to the beach and your friend Anna wants to come. Ask your parents.

....

21 I'd like ... / Would you like ... ?

Complete the sentences.

①
....
a biscuit?

②
....
two tickets, please.

③
....
buy this T-shirt.

④
....
come to my party?

Grammar reference

22 *have to* and *don't have to*

Positive			Negative			
I/You/We/They	**have to**	work.	I/You/We/They	**don't (do not)**	**have to**	work.
He/She/It	**has to**		He/She/It	**doesn't (does not)**		
Yes/No questions				**Short answers**		
Do	I/you/we/they	**have to**	work?	Yes, I/you/we/they **do**. No, I/you/we/they **don't**.		
Does	he/she/it			Yes, he/she/it **does**. No, he/she/it **doesn't**.		
Information questions						
When **do** we **have to finish** this work? Why **does** Ben **have to stay** at home?						

Monday: I have to get up early.

Sunday: I don't have to get up early.

- We use *have/has to* + verb for actions that are necessary.

  *I **have to** get up early on school days.*
  *My father **has to** work on Sundays.*
  ***Do** you **have to** do a lot of homework?*

- We use *don't/doesn't have to* + verb for actions that aren't necessary.

  *I **don't have to** get up early at the weekend.*
  *We **don't have to** wear a school uniform.*

23 Present perfect

Positive			Negative		
I/You/We/They	**'ve (have)**	**travelled** in Asia. **seen** this film.	I/You/We/They	**haven't (have not)**	**travelled** in Asia. **seen** this film.
He/She/It	**'s (has)**		He/She/It	**hasn't (has not)**	
Yes/No questions			**Short answers**		
Have	I/you/we/they	**travelled**? **seen** this film?	Yes, I/you/we/they **have**. No, I/ you/we/they **haven't**.		
Has	he/she/it		Yes, he/she/it **has**. No, he/she/it **hasn't**.		
Information questions					
What **have** you **done**? How many matches **have** they **won**? Which cities **has** he **visited**?					

- For the present perfect we use *have* + past participle.

- The past participle form of a verb is normally the same as the past simple.

  Regular: *They've **recorded** lots of songs.*   *He hasn't **played** volleyball before.*
  Irregular: *I've **met** your cousin.*   *Have you **heard** this song?*

- However, for some irregular verbs the past participle is different.

  *I've never **eaten** olives.*
  *She's **written** a book.*
  *Have you **seen** this painting?*

  ★ For a list of irregular verbs, see page 102.

- We use the present perfect to talk about events or experiences at some time in the past. We don't say exactly when they happened.

Grammar practice

22 have to and don't have to

Complete the sentences with the correct form of *have to*.

1 I .... be careful when I'm riding my bike here. There are always lots of cars on this road.

2 You can walk to the city centre from here. You .... take the bus.

3 Sonia is going to meet us later. She .... finish her homework first.

4 We .... hurry. We've got an hour before the film starts.

5 The temperature is sometimes –20°C here in the winter. People .... wear very warm coats, hats and boots.

6 A rugby player .... kick the ball. He can also pick it up and throw it.

7 A: .... students .... do exams at your school?

   B: Yes, they ....

8 A: .... your brother .... work at weekends?

   B: No, he ....

23 Present perfect

a Complete the sentences with the verbs in the present perfect.

1 Ellie ..has travelled.. (travel) around the world. She .... (visit) New York three times.

2 I .... (not meet) John but I .... (speak) to him on the phone.

3 He's a good director and he .... (make) lots of films, but he .... (not win) an Oscar.

4 A: .... you .... (learn) how to use the camera?

   B: Yes, but I .... (not take) many photos.

5 A: .... they .... (have) dinner?

   B: No, they .... (not eat) anything.

b Write the questions in the present perfect and then complete the answers.

1 you / listen / to this CD?

   ..Have you listened to this CD?..

   No, ..I haven't...

2 they / play / hockey before?

   ....

   Yes, ...

3 David / meet / your mother?

   ....

   Yes, ...

4 you / buy / anything from this shop?

   ....

   No, ...

5 Sophie / write / any emails to you?

   ....

   No, ...

Grammar reference

24 *going to*

Positive				Negative			
I	'm (am)	going to	leave.	I	'm not (am not)	going to	leave.
He/She/It	's (is)			He/She/It	isn't (is not)		
You/We/They	're (are)			You/We/They	aren't (are not)		
Yes/No questions				**Short answers**			
Am	I	going to	leave?	Yes, I **am**.	No, I**'m not**.		
Is	he/she/it			Yes, he/she/it **is**.	No, he/she/it **isn't**.		
Are	you/we/they			Yes, you/we/they **are**.	No, you/we/they **aren't**.		
Information questions							
When **are** you **going to ring** me? Where **are** we **going to stay**? What**'s** he **going to do** in the holidays?							

- The form is the verb *be* + *going to* + verb.

- We can also use these negative forms:
  You're not / We're not / They're not going to leave
  He's not / She's not / It's not going to leave

- We use *am/is/are* + *going to* + verb to talk about future plans and intentions.
  *I**'m going to buy** some shoes.*
  *She**'s going to phone** me later.*
  *I**'m not going to wash** my hair tonight.*
  *What **are** you **going to wear** to the party?*

25 *will* for offers and spontaneous decisions

Positive			Negative		
I/You/We/They/He/She/It	'll (will)	help.	I/You/We/They/He/She/It	won't (will not)	help.

- *Will* refers to the future.

- We use *I'll* + verb to make an offer to someone.
  *Don't worry about it. I**'ll help** you.*
  *Sit down and relax. I**'ll make** some tea.*

- We often use *I'll / I won't* + verb for decisions we've just made, a moment before speaking.
  *I think I**'ll wear** my blue jacket tonight.*
  *I **won't phone** Pete now. It's after 11 o'clock.*

Grammar practice

24 going to

a Complete the sentences. Use the verbs in the box with *going to.*

wear	wash	give	not study	not have	not wait

1 She _____ her hair.   4 They _____ it to their dad.

2 I _____ my black jeans.   5 I _____ a hamburger.

3 We _____ for you.   6 He _____ today.

b Write questions with *going to.*

1 I heard Jill is buying a car. *she / sell / her bike?*   <u>Is she going to sell her bike?</u>

2 Luis wants to talk to you. *you / phone him?*

3 A: I'm really sorry, Nick – I think I've lost your keys.

   B: Oh no! *What / I / do?*

4 A: Julia and Chris are taking the bus to the cinema.

   B: *What film / they / see?*

5 A: Silvio bought three new posters this morning.

   B: Yeah*? Where / he / put them?*

25 will for offers and spontaneous decisions

Complete the dialogues. Use *I'll* with a word from each box.

make	bring	go	now	~~to him tomorrow~~	to bed
get ready	~~talk~~		it to school tomorrow	some pasta	

1 A: We need to tell Greg about this.

   B: Yes, I know. <u>I'll talk to him tomorrow.</u>

2 A: Are you going to watch the film?

   B: No, I'm tired. I think _____

3 A: We have to leave in half an hour.

   B: Right. _____

4 A: I'm hungry, but it's too late to cook the chicken now.

   B: That's OK. _____

5 A: Did I leave my folder at your house?

   B: Yes, you did. _____

Irregular verbs

Verb	Past simple	Past participle	Verb	Past simple	Past participle
be	was/were	been	let	let	let
become	became	become	lose	lost	lost
begin	began	begun	make	made	made
blow	blew	blown	mean	meant	meant
break	broke	broken	meet	met	met
bring	brought	brought	pay	paid	paid
build	built	built	put	put	put
burn	burned/burnt	burned/burnt	read	read	read
buy	bought	bought	ride	rode	ridden
can	could	been able	ring	rang	rung
catch	caught	caught	run	ran	run
choose	chose	chosen	say	said	said
come	came	come	see	saw	seen
cost	cost	cost	sell	sold	sold
cut	cut	cut	send	sent	sent
do	did	done	set	set	set
draw	drew	drawn	shoot	shot	shot
drink	drank	drunk	shut	shut	shut
drive	drove	driven	sing	sang	sung
eat	ate	eaten	sit	sat	sat
fall	fell	fallen	sleep	slept	slept
feel	felt	felt	speak	spoke	spoken
fight	fought	fought	spell	spelled/spelt	spelled/spelt
find	found	found	spend	spent	spent
fly	flew	flown	stand	stood	stood
forget	forgot	forgotten	steal	stole	stolen
get	got	got	swim	swam	swum
give	gave	given	swing	swung	swung
go	went	gone	take	took	taken
grow	grew	grown	teach	taught	taught
have	had	had	tell	told	told
hear	heard	heard	think	thought	thought
hit	hit	hit	throw	threw	thrown
hold	held	held	understand	understood	understood
hurt	hurt	hurt	wake	woke	woken
keep	kept	kept	wear	wore	worn
know	knew	known	win	won	won
learn	learned/learnt	learned/learnt	write	wrote	written
leave	left	left			

Phonemic chart

Consonant sounds

/b/ bird

/tʃ/ cheese

/d/ door

/f/ fish

/g/ girl

/h/ heart

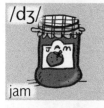
/dʒ/ jam

/k/ key

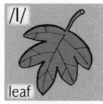
/l/ leaf

/m/ monkey

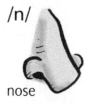
/n/ nose

/ŋ/ ring

/p/ pen

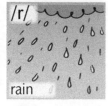
/r/ rain

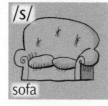
/s/ sofa

/ʃ/ shoe

/ʒ/ television

/t/ table

/ð/ feather

/θ/ think

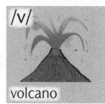
/v/ volcano

/w/ window

/j/ yoga

/z/ zoo

Vowel sounds

/æ/ apple

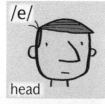
/e/ head

/i/ insect

/ɒ/ hot

/ʌ/ umbrella

/ʊ/ book

/ɑː/ arm

/ɜː/ earth

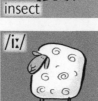
/iː/ sheep

/ɔː/ ball

/uː/ moon

/eə/ chair

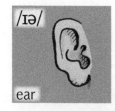
/ɪə/ ear

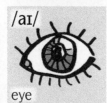
/aɪ/ eye

/eɪ/ paper

/ɔɪ/ boy

/əʊ/ phone

/aʊ/ owl

/ə/ computer

Go to the Interactive website to download the workbook audio.

www.cambridge.org/interactive

103